Praise for Front & Center Leadership

"Brandon leverages his years of experience in *Front & Center Leadership*, a guide packed with actionable steps to build your personal brand and become a modern leader who gets noticed. A great read for anyone looking to advance in their career."

Rah Mahtani, Head of Marketing - North America, Alibaba

"Building influence, credibility, and a recognizable voice can feel impossible looking forward from the middle of your career. *Front & Center Leadership* helps readers step into that role with a specific framework and insights from beloved influencers who have done just that."

Jenny Magic, Bestselling author of *Change Fatigue*

"If you've been hanging back and hesitating to start the journey of building your personal brand because you don't know where to start, start with Brandon Birkmeyer's book, *Front & Center Leadership*. Brandon acts as your guide, helping you with everything from initial shifts in your mindset to following a specific framework of actions to establish visibility, build authority, and make an impact on your community. A must-read for anyone looking to step into thought leadership."

Philip VanDusen, Former VP Head of Design at Pepsico, and host of the Brand Design Masters Podcast with 291K+ subscribers on YouTube

"All success starts with having a good relationship with yourself. *Front & Center Leadership* is an investment in your self-confidence, your self-awareness, and your communication. Brandon lays out simple ways to build your personal brand while developing the next level skills that will help you grow."

Travis Chappell, CEO, Guestio

"Personal branding is the great leadership skill you need—and few are taught. Thankfully, Brandon Birkmeyer has written this practical and story-filled guide to putting yourself front and center, so you can lead your organization to the front and center, too."

Tamsen Webster, Founder, Message Design Institute, and bestselling author of *Find Your Red Thread* and *Say What They Can't Unhear*

"Brandon is an experienced marketing professional with a significant perspective on building a personal brand as a modern leader. But what I like particularly love about this book is Brandon's genuine willingness to confront what held him back in the past and learn from it. It's not just a simple how-to, but rather a genuine look into how staying in the middle of the pack can create space between where you are now and where you want to be. *Front & Center Leadership* is a great guide to pushing through challenges with easy-to-follow step-by-step ideas and activities to build your reputation and influence."

Lauren V. Davis, CEO, Lauren Davis Creative, and host of The Real Personal Branding Podcast

"*Front & Center Leadership* is an essential read for leaders looking to elevate their personal brand. With his extensive experience at Coca-Cola and Apple, Brandon offers a practical, step-by-step framework filled with actionable activities and real-world success stories. This book is a valuable resource for anyone aiming to stand out and lead with confidence."

Neal Schaffer, Bestselling author of *The Age of Influence* and *Digital Threads*

"*Front & Center Leadership* is an epic guide for leaders who want to stand out through personal branding. Brandon Birkmeyer's expertise, interviews, and insights provide a clear roadmap for creating impactful content, building strong communities, and making a lasting impact in any industry. This book is a must-read for anyone looking to lead with purpose and authenticity."

Austin Armstrong, CEO, Syllabi.io, YouTuber 599K+ subscribers

"*Front & Center Leadership* by Brandon Birkmeyer makes a strong case for building your personal brand. This book provides a clear recipe for taking charge of your unique value and creating a compelling platform. Filled with activities, interviews, and insights, Brandon has crafted a veritable roadmap to guide you on your journey. Use it to stand out in a sea of sameness and elevate your leadership skills to new heights."

Stan Phelps, Certified Speaking Professional, and bestselling author of 15 business books including *Purple Goldfish 2.0*.

"*Front & Center Leadership* was a refreshing read. I was encouraged and inspired by Brandon's story and his journey to leadership through his brand. This book will encourage you to consider how you can take your own next steps toward building your personal brand strategically. Brandon lays out the why, the what, and the how to get started. Great read for anyone looking to elevate how they are impacting the world!"

Valerie Morris, CEO, Tintero Creative, and host of the Marketing Wins Podcast

"If you want to learn how to become a better leader in your industry, then you need to read *Front & Center Leadership*. Brandon provides you with a no-nonsense way of being intentional with how you lead your organization and how you lead through your brand. A must-read for marketing teams and the executive suite managing a large organization."

Kris Levy, Army Officer and Business Strategist

"*Front & Center Leadership* is a must-read for any ambitious professional looking to break out from the crowd and cement their reputation as a dynamic, purpose-driven leader. Brandon Birkmeyer masterfully articulates how leaders can harness the power of personal branding to take control of their narrative and differentiate themselves in today's competitive landscape. Packed with actionable insights and real-world examples, *Front & Center Leadership* is essential for any leader serious about elevating their personal brand and making a lasting impact. I highly recommend this book to anyone seeking to stand out, drive change, and advance their career."

Stephanie Garcia, Bestselling author of *The Ultimate Guide to Influencer Marketing*

"In today's fast-paced world, it's not enough to show up and do a great job. Leaders need to take ownership of their brands and careers, and that means getting intentional and making sure other people know who you are, what you do, and what you stand for. Building your personal brand has become an essential element of attracting the best talent and achieving future success and this book provides a great guide to help you do just that."

-Andy Storch, Bestselling author of *Own Your Career Own Your Life*, and host of The Talent Development Hot Seat Podcast

"Brandon provides practical wisdom on leveraging the power of your perspective to impact the people around you. This book gives leaders the tools they need to get discovered by their peers and recognized as a thought leader in their industry."

Grant Baldwin, Bestselling author of *The Successful Speaker*

FRONT& CENTER LEADERSHIP

HOW **LEADERS** USE **PERSONAL** **BRANDING** TO STAND OUT AND HOW YOU CAN TOO

BRANDON BIRKMEYER

Front & Center Leadership

How Leaders Use Personal Branding to Stand Out and How You Can Too

Copyright © 2024 by Brandon Birkmeyer

Published by Brands On Brands Inc.

This publication is designed to provide accurate and authoritative information in regard to the subject matter covered. It is sold with the understanding that neither the author nor the publisher is engaged in rendering legal, investment, accounting or other professional services. While the publisher and author have used their best efforts in preparing this book, they make no representations or warranties with respect to the accuracy or completeness of the contents of this book and specifically disclaim any implied warranties of merchantability or fitness for a particular purpose. No warranty may be created or extended by sales representatives or written sales materials. The advice and strategies contained herein may not be suitable for your situation. You should consult with a professional when appropriate. Neither the publisher nor the author shall be liable for any loss of profit or any other commercial damages, including but not limited to special, incidental, consequential, personal, or other damages.

ISBN 979-8-9907618-0-3 paperback | ISBN 979-8-9907618-2-7 ebook | ISBN 979-8-9907618-1-0 kindle

Book Cover by Brands On Brands Inc.

First Edition 2024

Dedication

To the strong and brilliant woman who leads our family,
my favorite person and loving wife, Jema.

To our two kids, Hannah and Jordan,
who are the center of our attention and affection.

To my parents, Barbara and Mike, who raised me
with heart, humility, humor, and hamburgers.

To all of our family and friends who have supported us
along the way and taught us what is really important.

FRONT&
CENTER
LEADERSHIP

Contents

INTRODUCTION

There are many qualified leaders out there who never lead. And, let's be honest, there are many people leading who shouldn't be. Getting a leadership position often takes initiative more than it takes skill. That creates a huge problem. Either, you have leadership skills and no one knows it or you have a leadership position but have never been given the proper training. The turning point for me came in my late thirties as my career started to require me to be more in the spotlight and to step into new skills.

Those skills lie somewhere at the intersection of leadership and personal branding. I needed to take more initiative. I had to be more outspoken and more communicative with key stakeholders. I needed to develop more industry relationships. I had to be a problem solver for my clients and a reputation builder for my company. To truly succeed, I couldn't hide. I had to be front and center in my career and in my life.

Not everyone wants to be front and center. I was willing to take the risk of putting myself out there. I was ready to be seen, and maybe judged, but definitely not ignored or overlooked. It was time to step up and stand out.

> The truth is that leadership doesn't come easy. You won't figure it out all at once, and will always be learning. You will often feel stuck in your progress and unnoticed in your achievements. Each day is a chance for you to learn something new, to push forward, and figure it out.

When I started drafting this book, I was not sure if it should be classified as a personal branding book or a leadership book. There are already so many books about personal branding and even more about leadership. Despite all the books that exist on both subjects, I still have a lengthy list of things I wish someone would have told me when I was younger. At first, I did not know if my ideas were worth sharing or if my book would add any value.

I was motivated to keep going as I reminded myself that my voice is unique to me and that I am sharing ideas that would have helped the younger me. That younger me was ambitious to elevate my skills and to grow in my career, always seeking a challenge. But the path forward wasn't always obvious.

Leadership seemed like some far-off thing that I aspired to achieve. It was a goal way out on the horizon. Knowing what I know now, there are three critical skills I would have invested in much earlier in my life to help me get ahead. Those three skills are communication, relationship building, and problem-solving. These are the skills that I've seen build reputation the fastest. Developing your reputation is at the heart of personal branding, but it's not enough to make you a leader. It only qualifies you.

If you're reading this book, it means you're the type who wants to figure it out. When you hit a wall or get stuck, you put in the work. You force yourself to get unstuck. You see the value in stepping up and taking initiative, even when feeling reluctant or lacking motivation. You are on a journey to step up, stand out, and lead, and I'm here to help.

This book focuses on two character-defining behaviors:

- Stepping up to the front of the line – Being first, taking initiative, and overcoming reluctant behavior.

- Standing out as the center of attention – Finding your voice as a leader, and building your reputation with intention.

I believe stepping up and standing out are the secret ingredients to emerging as a recognized leader in your organization and industry. I call this **Front and Center Leadership**.

This may not be a "popular" opinion. Stepping up to the front of the line sounds selfish, but being a leader requires you to volunteer yourself to lead.

Standing out as the center of attention sounds arrogant, but being a leader requires you to be seen, to have a point of view, and to share it.

It is popular to tell people to be patient and polite, but isn't it your turn yet? You get to decide when to step up. You are highly deserving, but you are waiting for a turn which may never come. You were told that seeking attention is a terrible thing, but too many great leaders like you are going unnoticed or being overlooked.

You can keep waiting, but it's never going to happen on its own. Waiting sucks, and it's getting in your way. It's popular to tell people to fit in and be humble, but stepping up and standing out is a differentiator. It separates you from the crowd. It pushes you forward, past fear and doubt. It is the spark that creates opportunities, both in business and in life.

And, by the way, you don't have to step on other people to get ahead. But you do need to step out of the crowd and be front and center for your next leadership opportunity to begin.

If you would like to download a free companion guide to *Front & Center Leadership* complete with personal branding exercises, editable worksheets, and examples, go to BrandonBirkmeyer.com/FCL

PART 1

The Path to Leadership

Chapter One

My Front & Center Journey

During my twenty years in advertising, I paid my dues and climbed the corporate ladder. I spent most of my career working in the media planning departments of large advertising agencies. I worked my way up from assistant-level positions to become a director of media, leading brand strategy at top agencies in Los Angeles and New York. Many of my clients were Fortune 100 companies, and I am proud of my resume.

Despite the tremendous success I generated for myself and the companies I worked for, I hit a ceiling when it came to earning a seat at the executive leadership table. I had no idea how long it would take. There were very few top-level positions, and they very rarely became vacant.

When a position did become available, there were always people ahead of me in line, with more experience and more years at the company. They had also waited and waited, and their turn was long overdue. **Success was determined by patience, not performance.**

Eventually, I got tired of waiting for someone else to give me a turn. During the last five years of my career, I was enamored with the idea of starting my own marketing company. I bought website domains, laid out business plans, and dreamed about one day being my own boss. I started to take on freelance work and then eventually took the plunge into entrepreneurship.

As soon as I left my job, I had a shocking realization: I had a resume but no reputation. I had colleagues but no network. I had experience and skills but not the *right* skills. I did not know how to demonstrate my worth or how to create value for others. I had no authority, influence, or proven value.

I thought that small business owners and entrepreneurs would be interested in working with me because I had years of professional marketing experience. But I didn't know any entrepreneurs. More specifically, they didn't know me. I had no history of working with entrepreneurs. I had not proven that I could solve any problems they were facing.

I hit this wall, but I was starting to understand my problem. I had a bad habit of overthinking things, and I wanted everything to be perfect before I put myself out there. Most people who hit this wall feel lost. I'll admit, I was a little discouraged in the beginning.

On the bright side, there was something else I was feeling that I had not experienced before. It was a feeling of clarity. For the first time in forever, I knew exactly what barriers I had to overcome and the steps I needed to take to achieve my goals.

The great news was that I didn't have to wait my turn. I could immediately start taking action. When I was in a corporate job, the only solution I could see was to continue waiting. But in entrepreneurship, there is no waiting. Action is required for success. So that's what I did. I found three critical actions that I could focus on to help me build a business.

Before I talk about those three actions, I want to mention one thing. These actions aren't just for entrepreneurs. In fact, if I had taken these same three actions while in my corporate job, I know that I would have been more successful at breaking into the executive leadership circle. But I didn't know what I didn't know.

Entrepreneurship allowed me to step outside of my work and career path to analyze myself and my actions. In my career, I received regular feedback and annual performance reviews, but I never found any steps I could take to set myself apart from my colleagues.

As an employee for ad agencies, I saw myself as a team player and a contributor to a bigger picture, but as an entrepreneur, I started to look at myself as a product and a brand, and the steps became obvious.

These steps I'm about to share can work for you too, whether you are an entrepreneur or an employee. Yes, even as an employee, you can be a team player and a brand at the same time.

But first, you must change how you view yourself. You must realize that you are a product with your own brand that is being leveraged on your company's behalf, and you can also be wielding your brand on your own behalf.

How to Build a Personal Brand

To build your personal brand with intention, there are three critical actions to take. I call these *The Personal Branding Framework*.

Here's how it works:

1. **Create content** and share ideas that demonstrate your expertise

2. **Build a community** of friends, partners, and clients that you can serve

3. **Make an impact** by solving problems and adding value

Think of this book as the roadmap for building your reputation. I will lead you through The Personal Branding Framework, breaking down each action in detail along with prioritized steps for you to take in the beginning and beyond.

Every step in this book comes from personal experience as well as from the minds of the amazing people I've met on my journey. As a content creator, podcaster, blogger, and YouTuber, I have the opportunity to interview some of my favorite marketers, authors, keynote speakers, entrepreneurs, and thought leaders. I am sharing their personal branding stories and advice as examples within this book.

Let me say one thing before we dive in. I want you to know that anyone can do this. You are the driver of your reputation. Every action you take contributes to your success, and there is no deadline. Every day is a new day to contribute to your life's work, which is you! There's no better way to spend your time and effort than to invest in your own personal development and reputation.

Your journey starts with being able to choose the right path to take and identifying your priorities. When the path is clear, it's just a matter of taking action. Now, taking action isn't as easy as it sounds. If it were easy, we'd all be doing it.

But it's not all about your conscious choices. For me, understanding the forces behind my reluctance and initiative was a critical step on the journey. I know it will be critical for your journey as well. So, in this book, we'll dive into those topics as well to give you the mindset and self-awareness you'll need to implement what you learn from these chapters.

Finding Your Small Window of Opportunity

If you need a little more inspiration to get you moving, look at the actions you took during some of the biggest moments in your life. Whether in school or in a job, or in your friendships and relationships, there will have been small windows of opportunity that changed your life, triggered by your own actions. Something drives you to take those actions. Something moves you to do something different or even extraordinary.

It's happened to me many times in my life, but I didn't always pay attention to it. Or I thought it happened *to me* instead of believing that I was a part of making it happen. The truth is that finding those small windows of opportunity changed the trajectory of my life (more than once).

One of the biggest moments of my life started with something completely out of my control. My girlfriend of almost two years had accepted a new job that would move her out of Los Angeles and across the country to New York City. It was a major life change for her that had also upended my world.

She gave her two weeks' notice to her job in Los Angeles and to me on the same day. It was a dream job in her dream city, but to me, it was a nightmare. My world was crushed. In my mind, this girl might be *the one,* and we'd often talked about what our futures together could look like. But that was all going to disappear, and there was nothing I could do about it.

I thought maybe we could try to do a long-distance relationship, but that was not something she was interested in. It was *get married* or *goodbye.* And that ended our relationship, or so I thought.

Of course, the story doesn't end there. This is a story about taking action and big moments. It's not about inaction and paths we wished we had taken. But remember, these are the lessons I wish I had known when I was younger.

I did not chase the girl. I was not bold. I did not quit my job, pack my things, and follow her. I did nothing.

For six months, I just lived my life and let life happen *to me*. I followed my daily routine and waited to see how things would play out. Maybe I'd meet someone new. Maybe she'd come back. Lots of maybes and more waiting.

As you can imagine, this was not a very fulfilling life. I was in denial about how I felt, but I went through all the emotions: angry that she left, betrayed, and abandoned. I was numb, trying to pretend it never happened.

But it did happen, and it wasn't going to change unless I did something about it. Then I got lucky. That same girl started a blog about her experiences in New York City. I couldn't help myself and was reading it each week. One of the weeks, six months after we had broken up, she wrote a blog addressed to me and our old relationship. I found my small window of opportunity. I had a chance to get this relationship back, but that window was closing fast.

It was a Wednesday morning, and after some back and forth in my brain, I found twenty seconds of courage and sent her a message. The only thing that I typed in the message was, "Hey." I didn't overthink it. I just sent it. I had no plans, just the feeling that I wanted to reach out and connect with her. The next few hours were torture. She didn't respond to me for almost three hours.

When she finally wrote back, I didn't have much to say. I knew I needed to do something, not say something. I asked her what she was doing at midnight on Friday. It was Wednesday, and the first flight I could catch to New York City arrived Friday at midnight. She said she was willing to meet for coffee, so I booked the flight.

That small window of opportunity changed my life. In that moment, I decided to quit my job and move across the country. Two weeks later, we were back together, and I was in New York City for job interviews and to find an apartment. One year later, I proposed marriage to her in a helicopter flying over that same city. One year after that, we were married. One year later, we had our first child. And our story continues to write itself. All because I stepped up in one moment.

I am telling you this story to show you the power of initiative. **Even small actions can change your life.** Anyone can find twenty seconds of courage. I'm not a risk taker. I prefer to play it safe when I can, but I'm tired of waiting. I now see that I can find the inspiration to act given the right circumstances and a little clarity, and you can too.

> In this book, I share my views on the initiative and the mindset you need to take action in building your reputation. You'll be prompted with exercises to get you started. You'll find some chapters include "Activity Breaks" to help you put the concepts into action.

Think of this book as a step-by-step plan to audit your actions, set priorities, and make decisions about where you want to step up and stand out in your life. I also cover some ways to break your routines, develop better habits, and overcome any reluctance holding you back.

I hope that this book inspires you to rethink your reputation, step out of the crowd, recognize your worth, and live your life *front* and *center*.

Chapter Two

What is Front & Center Leadership?

F ront and Center Leadership is the consistent act of stepping up and standing out with intention. Stepping up to the front of the line and standing out as the center of attention.

When you step up to the front of the line, you are telling the world that you know your worth and you have confidence in your opinions. You are willing to try new things and be first. You are present and engaged. You are willing to take risks that align with your values. You are willing to take the responsibility of leading others.

When you stand out as the center of attention, you're the person that tells the world you have something to say that's worth paying attention to. You know the power of your perspective and are willing to share it and be seen. You are not afraid of other people's opinions.

Front and Center Leadership is the willingness to step up and stand out in the service of others. It's the combination of initiative and personal branding with intention.

Why Does Front and Center Leadership Matter?

There are lots of books, blogs, and research about the skills that are important once you reach a leadership position. According to a McKinsey analysis of academic literature as well as a survey of nearly two hundred thousand people in eighty-one organizations all over the world[1], there are four types of behavior that account for eighty-nine percent of leadership effectiveness:

1. Being supportive

2. Operating with a strong results orientation

3. Seeking different perspectives

4. Solving problems effectively

But the people who should be leaders already have these skills. Whether these skills come naturally to you or you developed them over time, you are already leadership material. The truth is that highly capable and deserving people are often overlooked and are sometimes reluctant to lead.

You may have legitimate reasons to be reluctant about pursuing the next-level leadership position. A common fear is that pursuing leadership positions may negatively affect your current relationships. You worry that you'll appear to be aggressive or pushy. You may get blamed if something goes wrong. Or you're afraid that you're not qualified enough.

Any of these reasons may be enough to hold some people back. But not you. You are done waiting. You are ready to step up and stand out.

Here are some characteristics that you'll need to lean on to show Front and Center Leadership.

You Have Ambition

You are someone who has an idea of what they want from their career, from their life, and from their business. To get there, you must be willing to take the necessary steps and put yourself in a position to grab those opportunities.

You don't want reluctance to get in your way, but reluctance is a sneaky adversary because you don't always know when it's happening. If I asked you today, "Are you ready to be promoted to your next position?" most of you would say, "Yes, I'm ready. Give it to me!"

However, that is usually not how it's asked. Usually, it's a hundred little steps across the year to make an impression. Those little steps determine whether you're going to wait for something to happen to you or whether you're going to act. Reluctance rears its head in those moments where you are waiting your turn; when you are waiting for someone else to have the idea first, to see what the consensus is.

Waiting is the problem. There are many things out of your control, but you can't keep waiting for leadership to happen to you. You must be actively taking steps toward it. You have ambition, but you need to act, step up, and take the initiative to put yourself in that first position and create the opportunity.

This is how you go from being absent to being present in all your daily interactions.

You have ambition. Stop waiting for leadership to happen to you.

You Are Unique

You are special and different from other people in your world. You don't want to be like everyone else, and that's okay!

Someone who's unique should be ready and willing to show that. You must be happy to stand out and not be a commodity in your organization, industry, and life. There's lots of competition out in the world and a lot of things make you comparable to other people. It's time to share your uniqueness.

You are ready to add value in a way that makes you stand out. Finding that value—finding that different way to show up that sets you apart from the competition—is what Front and Center Leadership is all about. This is how you move forward in an organization, in your life, and in your business.

You Are Ready for Change

You seek out change. Yes, we all have our routines, but if you are ready for change, then you know that it's your time for something different. You're prepared and excited for that, but change doesn't happen all by itself. You must be the agent of that change.

How you spend your time every day is what determines what change happens to you. You may be ready for change, but change will not happen without some type of inciting act. When a door opens, you must have cultivated the skills, answered the questions, taken on the challenges, even when not asked to, so you can be the person that someone's looking for in that next position.

You Can Figure It Out

You know what's next. You don't have to wait for someone to tell you what to do. In fact, no one is going to tell you what to do, and no one is going to do it for you. Only *you* can create momentum in your life. This is why taking the initiative is so important.

When you don't know what to do next, the easy thing is to do nothing or to fill your life with the normal things that you do every day—to stick to the normal parts of your routine, the assignments that your bosses or client provide, and the normal tasks that are part of your job.

It's time to break your routines and go beyond what's normal. Move forward by figuring out your own next step. Map out the path that leads to your growth.

To grow, you may need to change how you think. You are ready to think in a new way that is more challenging and developmental. Actively seek out opportunities for growth. Think about what you need to do next. Choose the skills that you are going to work on. You can always get better at challenging yourself to take on more responsibility, to take on new and unfamiliar paths.

You can figure out what's next. You just need enough curiosity to do that, and it is up to you.

Find out where you are on your personal brand journey. Take the quiz and get your own brand scorecard! Go to BrandonBirkmeyer.com/FCL.

---

1. https://www.mckinsey.com/featured-insights/mckinsey-explainers/what -is-leadership

Chapter Three

The "Middle of the Pack" Mentality

I believe it's true that you can have anything you want in life, but you must be willing to go after it. You must make the choice to chase it. If that's true, why aren't we all chasing our dreams? Going after what you want can be simple, but it's not easy.

Let me ask you this. The last time you were at a comedy show, did you choose to be in the front row near the comedian? Or in the middle of the room with the crowd. Most people sit in the middle. Why is that? Well, you're naturally programmed to avoid attention and standing out. You move toward the safety of the middle of the pack.

You know that if you sit in the front row, the comedian has the opportunity to engage with you. They will see you. They might have a reason to shine the light on you, to put attention and focus on you as part of the routine, and that makes you uncomfortable. It makes you reluctant to make the decision to be in the front.

Reluctance is a powerful force against leadership. You must be able to move past reluctance and find the will and the drive to act. You must find your own innate initiative. **Initiative is simply the act of moving first.** It's the choice to move first toward your goal.

What's challenging about initiative is that you typically have reasons to be reluctant. You have legitimate, often experienced or known, reasons to be reluctant about a situation.

But it's more complicated than that. There are decisions you make or don't make every day that are driven by reluctance. You are consciously or unconsciously held back from moving forward, taking risks, or stepping up and standing out, all because of this crazy thing called reluctance.

As I reflected on my own reluctance, I realized that not all reluctance is the same. There are different types of reluctance that can show up in your daily life.

In fact, there are three types which we'll discuss in this book:

- Classic reluctance – Playing it safe

- Thoughtful indecision – Weighing all the options

- Agreeableness – Going with the flow

Classic Reluctance

The first type of reluctance is the most common, and we'll call this *classic reluctance*. This is your standard, "I don't want to," or, "I'm afraid to," response to any given situation. In the previous example of going to a comedy show, if you are considering sitting in the front row, you may think to yourself, "I don't want to be the butt of the joke tonight," or, "I don't want the attention tonight," or, "I'm afraid that something will come up and I'll feel embarrassed."

You have legitimate, thoughtful reasons for not wanting to do something. You may also recognize that there could be benefits to going against that fear and moving past it. For example, if you choose to sit in the front row at the comedy show, you may be more engaged or involved in the act and have more fun. It might be a more memorable night if that comedian brings attention to you. It might improve the experience, but that reluctance can hold you back from considering it.

That's one specific example, but this happens in a lot of situations. In a meeting, in a job, or in a business decision, you may have reluctance. You are either afraid of the risk involved or uncertain as to what the outcome may be of that decision.

Often, that reluctance comes from a preformed opinion, preference, or even fear. ***Classic reluctance* is your way of playing it safe.**

Thoughtful Indecision

The second type of reluctance, which I think happens to me a lot, is *thoughtful indecision*. It is slightly different to *classic reluctance*, but it's just as effective at slowing us down.

With *thoughtful indecision*, you are actively contemplating whether you should or should not move forward and act. And that decision-making process slows you down to the point of complete stagnation. You are paralyzed.

They call it analysis paralysis for a reason. You get stuck weighing all the pros and cons. You continue to add reasons for and reasons against with no end in sight. In that analysis, you come up with reasons to delay a decision because you're not ready, or you don't have enough information, or you are still thinking about the outcomes and aren't sure how you feel about them.

You are being thoughtful, but you are still reluctant to act. *Thoughtful indecision* can result in you losing out. When you are ready to make that decision to move forward, it's too late. You lose the opportunity because of the time delay in making that decision.

That is just as big of a problem as anything else because you are losing the opportunity. You did not act fast enough, and someone else made the decision quicker than you because they didn't hesitate. ***Thoughtful indecision* leaves you stuck weighing all the options.**

Agreeableness

The last type of reluctance, *agreeableness*, could happen unconsciously more than anything else. This is the go-with-the-flow type of situation. With *agreeableness*, you either think you don't really care about the outcome of a situation or you do care but not enough to fight for it.

Agreeableness can get us into a lot of trouble because the outcomes of those moments can be detrimental to our future. Any time a decision is made for you, you risk that it doesn't align with your goals or values. *Agreeableness* places other people's priorities above your own, and in the end, you're not doing yourself any favors.

This can happen in a group situation where you and other people are trying to compromise to come up with a decision. This can include negotiation, persuasion, or lots of conversation. This can involve voting on something.

Instead of presenting what your opinion is and taking the lead, you are compliant. Rather than having a perspective and putting a stake in the ground, pitching your case, you sit back and let other people make the decision for you.

You are afraid of what other people think of you. You don't want to be seen as disagreeable. ***Agreeableness* forces you to go with the flow.**

> Most corporations are consensus-driven machines. Leaders are valued because they share their unique perspectives with conviction. Your perspective is your power. If no one hears your perspective, then it doesn't get considered. And maybe your perspective was the right one for the moment in time, either for the group or for yourself.

Taking initiative, or overcoming reluctance, is not complicated. It's not easy either! But it's not complicated.

Taking initiative simply means that you are willing to take action first toward your goals. And what I would encourage is that you find what those situations are that would be most important for you as a place to start.

Chapter Four

The Roadmap to Reputation

Your reputation is always with you, but it's not something you often think about. You go through your days, year after year, having experiences, working, playing, living your life, and along the way, your reputation is building, growing, changing, and adapting.

But you don't often stop to think about what your reputation says about you. How do you make it better? What has caused your reputation to be what it is right now? To actively manage your reputation, you must develop a reputation-building mindset. To move your reputation to where you want it to be, you must actively think about what you are doing and what you need to do.

To do that, there are questions that you can ask yourself every year, every quarter, or at any point in time to create a roadmap for your reputation:

- Where have you been?

- Where are you right now?

- Where do you want to go?

Look at Where You Have Been

When you look at where you've been, start with your own history and experience. If you go back in time, especially when you are looking to build a reputation, start by looking at your skills, work history, and any other experiences that might add up to something that is an opinion driver for your personal brand.

The same tactics work whether you are building a career or growing your own business. If you're an independent entrepreneur, all those skills and experiences are things that people look at to answer, "Is this person right for me?"

Take the time to list out those skills and experiences. Write down the experiences you've had on a timeline. Those experiences could be jobs or projects and roles within each job. They could be certain accolades you are proud of or skills that you picked up. Then make a chart that looks at those things. Identify your peaks and your valleys.

Yes, you should also pay attention to the bad experiences. From every bad experience, there's something you have learned. The wins and the losses become stories along the way. They are examples of how your reputation developed. Most entrepreneurs will tell you that their biggest failures were their greatest learning moments and crucial turning points in their business.

Even if you don't have your own business, you can benefit from thinking like an entrepreneur. Start to keep a record of your experiences, not just a resume. Include all the reputational experiences that you have along the way.

When you have a record of your reputational experiences, it is easier to be confident in your ability to change and grow. You'll notice you have already used your thoughts and actions to help the people around you. As you are remembering those ideas and documenting those experiences, you can also start to ponder the question: *Who are you?*

The question of who you are is usually one that holds people up. It sounds like: *What's your purpose?* or *why do you exist on this earth?* But that's not where we're going.

Who you are is simply all your intentions and experiences added up until they start to define you as a person. I like to think about this broken down into job categories and primary skills. So, for me, as someone whose experience has mostly been in the business world and the marketing space, I am a marketer. I could use other words as well. I worked in media planning, so I'm a planner. I worked in brand strategy, so I'm a brand strategist. I worked in advertising, so I'm an advertising professional.

The more you can document this and get comfortable with using the different terms and terminology, the better you will be at explaining and introducing yourself to other people. And that's the key—other people. Who you are is only relevant after you start to figure out who you are for.

For example, when I meet one type of person, I might introduce myself with one title versus another depending on who they are and what information is most relevant to them. If I go to a parents' group meeting, I'm no longer identified by my career. I am now identified as the father of two children of certain ages and grade levels whose kids are in certain sports and who participates in certain parenting activities. That's the information that's relevant to that person.

If I'm at a leadership meeting, I talk about my leadership experience. At a meeting with other speakers, I discuss my speaking experience. At a meeting with content creators, I share my content creation experience. You must adapt your experiences to the environment you're in. Who you are will be the sum of all your different titles and experiences shared in a way that someone would understand.

Look at Where You Are Now

Today, you have a very specific set of skills and years of experience that allow you to operate in a certain way. How you serve people, your professional delivery, and the way you act are all defined by your experience. When you apply for job opportunities, they ask about your previous jobs and the length of time you spent at those jobs. They want to know if your experience is relevant and if it's aligned with the job. They want to know if you are someone who is a beginner, in the middle, or at the end of your career.

Just like a business exists as a startup versus a growing business with a slightly more solid foundation versus a large enterprise business. Start to think about yourself and where you fit in that way.

One way to frame that is to think about who you help and how you help them right now. The answer is determined by all the people that you run across every day. That includes your bosses, your coworkers, and the people whose businesses work with yours.

As a brand strategist, my role included doing consumer research, evaluating marketing opportunities, creating strategic plans, and client management. Each of these tasks were ways that I helped people. When I was in that role, the problems I solved depended on the situation, but a lot of the time, I was providing strategic planning or marketing recommendations. Some roles will always stand out more than others. Just look at the people you are helping to figure out what problem you solve.

> For entrepreneurs, this is easy. They do this all the time. That's how they built their business. They found a place in the market with a problem they could solve, and they solved it. As you're transitioning from resume to reputation, taking an entrepreneurial approach might help you clarify your identity.

Your reputation contributes to your personal brand, and your mindset helps you be better prepared to act toward your goals. Here's a quick example.

Let's say you have clients that you work with every day. Those clients have a set of goals as well as their own strengths, weaknesses, and challenges. Identify the different ways that you could help them while building your personal brand. Track the things that you could do to make your work with them more productive, effective, and cost-efficient. Think about all the different ways you could help your client. Then act and become known as someone who solves certain types of problems.

Other stakeholders to consider are people within your organization. Identify how you can help your organization build its reputation, while building your own. For example, getting out there and becoming a thought leader for your organization or helping to develop a report, article, or a white paper for your organization can be something that benefits both of you. You take the lead on it. Your name is on it, but so is the organization's. And now you have the skill of developing this kind of work. These ideas can be mutually beneficial.

Start to think about who your audience is. **Every person has an audience, whether we like it or not.** Your clients are your audience. Your coworkers at your organization are your audience. And lastly, you have your industry as a potential audience.

Most of my career was spent in the advertising industry. My clients were often in different industries than me. I worked with many clients in retail, financial services, consumer packaged goods, home goods, automotive services, and many more. Anyone I encountered across those many industries could be considered my audience. Building my reputation meant being aware of how they saw me—as a peer, a thought leader in the industry, or just another advertising guy. You get to control how you show up.

Your reputation is measured by your clients, your organization, and your industry; and then you have your teammates in the organization. You need to be aware of how you show up for them. Do not underestimate the value of being a team player. Help develop key talent or your teams. Build a reputation as the person who brings your team together, a great communicator. Be the person who supports others in getting their jobs done. All these things start to develop a reputation around who you are as a person in that organization.

So, I'll ask you again, who do you help? You might have multiple answers, but think about them, write them down, and develop a plan to help. What problems do they need solved? And where do you feel pulled to want to help? Because you're going to have passion and curiosity around that topic. You're going to be proud of the work that you do when it aligns with who you are.

Look at Where You Are Going

When looking at where you are going, you can get confused if you are not sure where you want to go.

All you've thought about are your personal goals. Maybe you want to move up one level in your organization and eventually lead that organization. If you're an entrepreneur, maybe you want more sales, better clients, and more lifestyle freedom. Or perhaps you're just trying to keep your career or business afloat, and you haven't thought about where you want to go.

To think about where you want to go, you need to identify who you want to become and why it matters to you. For example, in your organization, if you want to solve problems for your clients, you might have to look at yourself and honestly evaluate if you have the skills to do that effectively.

Or maybe there are problems you want to solve but aren't positioned to do so yet. You may know how to be helpful, but first you must focus on becoming known as the person that can solve those problems.

Take charge of your career growth by building a list of goals based on the skills you need to grow. Start by looking at the leaders in your organization and determining what skills have helped them get to the top. For example, you can work on getting better at things like writing, public speaking, communicating, team management, relationships, charisma, networking, or thought leadership. As you start to expose yourself to more of that information, you can decide what skills you want to improve and how you get there.

After evaluating where you've been, where you are right now, and where you are going, you must figure out why it matters to you.

> This is important. That motivation is what's going to drive you to continue to be curious and do the work. You need motivation because it's easy to fall back into your routines. It's easy to avoid or delay those initial steps to grow, to expand your knowledge, and to push yourself to become better. You will only be successful in your career, business, or life goals if they matter to you.

Your reasons are going to be different than someone else's. Start to get more connected to your motivations. Beyond your survival needs, look at your lifestyle goals. If you're not there yet, that's okay. But if you've already met some of those survival needs and you're starting to feel bored or disconnected from your work, it might mean that you need to reevaluate your motivations and look for a deeper purpose in the work that you're doing.

In summary, when creating a reputation-building mindset, there are three things you're looking at:

- Where have you been?

- Where are you right now?

- Where do you want to go?

Answer those questions. Look at the skills you've developed in the past and figure out who you want to help right now and how you can help. Then work toward that vision.

You are now on the path of developing a reputation-building mindset that'll push you toward your goals and help you build your personal brand.

Head over to BrandonBirkmeyer.com/FCL to download your copy of The Personal Branding Workbook. You'll get worksheets to answer questions from each of the chapters and step-by-step guides and checklists to keep you moving.

Activity Break: Audit Yourself

Get started with a self-audit of your own history and set your future goals. Here are a few places to start.

These worksheets are available at BrandonBirkmeyer.com/FCL.

Your History

- What are some key experiences, skills, and accomplishments in your past that have shaped your reputation?

- Can you identify any significant peaks or valleys in your journey that have influenced your reputation?

- What are your current skills, experiences, and roles?

- How do you currently serve others in your professional life and personal life?

Your Goals

- What are your career goals and personal goals?

- Why do these goals matter to you personally?

- What skills or qualities do you need to develop to achieve these goals?

- How can you align your future aspirations with your current reputation and skill set?

- Who are the key audiences or stakeholders you interact with on a regular basis?

PART 2
The Personal Branding Framework

Chapter Five

What is The Personal Branding Framework

Personal branding is more than your reputation. **Personal branding is the act of developing your reputation with *intention*.** Your reputation defines how people see you, approach you, and eventually want to do business with you. If you're reading this book, you already know that you have a say in your reputation. You have ownership of your personal brand.

Your personal brand is how you represent yourself to the world. If you are looking for a promotion, your personal brand will be a big part of your company's decision-making process. If you are starting a business or you're thinking about starting a business, your personal brand will help you establish business relationships and find customers. For example, if you want to be a coach or a mentor or provide some kind of service, your personal brand helps you become known and get found by the right people who need your service.

As an entrepreneur, there are a few things you can do to develop an effective personal brand. First, make sure that you are well-positioned in the market. In other words, show and tell people what you do, how you do it, and why it's the right choice for them. Explain to people why you are different and what makes them right for your service. Show them how you can help them.

This is about figuring out who you are. When starting on your personal branding journey, ask yourself how you want to help people. Clarify what you are looking to offer. These are simple distinctions, but it's normal to struggle with clarity in the beginning because of the fear of failure. You worry that you won't sound good enough or be different enough. Or you worry that you won't be chosen by your audience.

> There is room for you in your market, in your industry, and in your world. There are people waiting for you and your service—people who will choose you because they connect with you better than with other people. At all times, your ideas and your personal brand are attracting the right people for you and repelling the rest.

Figure out the thing you want to do to help people. The answer comes from you, not from them. Don't ask everyone else's opinion on what they think you should offer. It starts with you, your skills, your experience, and your interest in solving specific problems for specific people. Think about how to choose your category of work. Determine what you can start helping people with today. Then start talking to people about that and finding ways to help them.

When building your personal brand, you are working toward three outcomes. Each of the outcomes requires its own set of actions. The Personal Branding Framework aligns those outcomes with the actions you need to take to get there:

- Action #1 Creating content... leads to Outcome #1 Authority

- Action #2 Building community... leads to Outcome #2 Influence

- Action #3 Making an impact... leads to Outcome #3 Credibility

Your content creates authority in your niche. It demonstrates your expertise, accumulates, and becomes a larger archive.

Your community creates influence with your fans. It connects you to the people that want to follow you. It shifts from you being around others to you directly leading them.

Your impact builds credibility as you create value for others. It grows and becomes something that can be systematized and modeled out to help more people.

All of this contributes to your personal brand. Your personal brand will always be growing and changing; it's never done. You can always create more content, build more community, and make more impact. The potential of your personal brand is limitless and ever-expanding.

Start with small, simple steps. Figure out how to help one person today with something small. Work on one idea for how you help people. Express yourself. Share one opinion, one thought, one comment.

Get started!

Creating Content

A personal brand starts with who you are and what you put out into the world. Creating content helps you become known as a thought leader in your industry and separates you from the crowd. Here are three questions to help you get clear on what content you should create.

- Who are the key audiences and decision-makers?

- What do you want to be known for?

- How do you like to express yourself?

This takes you from looking at the internal decisions and ideas in your head to looking at an external audience instead. Who are the key audiences and decision-makers in your life, in your business, or at work? It's great to have ideas and to be putting in work, but figure out who that work is for.

You might have multiple audiences and decision-makers to be thinking about. This could be your peers or the people you work with. What do you need to do around them to be different, to stand out, to step up? How do you stand out to your own peers?

Another audience might be your direct bosses. How do you stand out to your bosses? How do they notice the work you're doing in a positive way?

Another audience might be management and other leaders in your organization. How do you stand out to them? Find ways to get noticed amongst the larger crowd of the organization. And then look at other audiences, such as partners of the organization or key vendors of the organization. Build better, more prominent relationships with them as well.

And stand out to the clients or customers of the organization as someone who is a leader. Be someone who is notably different than the rest of the organization. Make an impact on these people based on what their needs are and how you can serve them.

All of this adds up to building your personal brand. Figure out who those audiences are so that you can understand what motivates them and what you can do to stand out to them.

Then, figure out what you want to be known for. You can be known for your behavior, personality, ideas, and actions. That might vary by audience.

To your boss, you might want to be seen as leadership material or a great team manager. You want them to trust you with big projects for your clients. You might want to be known for making their lives easier, being productive, and helping them better understand the landscape of the business. To your peers, you might want to be known as a team player who always has great ideas and steps up to lead the group.

Moving from unknown to known takes active consideration and vision for what you want to be known for. This doesn't happen by accident. You decide who your key audiences are and who to lead. What do you need to be doing in front of them? What actions do you need to be taking so that they can see those ideas, actions, and behaviors?

But first, start with that vision of what you want to be known for. Have that clearly defined and written out.

Once you pick the audience and your topic, it's time to figure out how you like to express yourself. You can either:

- Curate content – Collect and share top industry news and opinions

- Create conversations – Interview industry experts

- Provide commentary – Share your point of view on relevant and trending content happening around your topic

Content curation involves collecting different news, trends, and opinions from your industry as a source and sharing it on your platform with a little bit of reporting or announcing on top of it. It's a great way to get started if you haven't yet identified your exact perspective in your industry. Expressing yourself and at least calling out that these are the big things that seem to matter right now in your industry is a good start. It gets you into the habit of content creation. Plus, you get to **test your ideas and see what resonates most with you and your audience** over time.

Conversations bring you and another person together to discuss something happening in your industry, and it's one of the easiest ways to create content today. It can be in person or on paper, through a live interview or via written questions and answers. It can be a podcast, a YouTube video, or a blog, but basically, it's you and another person talking about your industry.

These conversations can be broken into different formats. You could be the interviewer and they could be the expert, or you can both be sharing ideas around a topic that you are facilitating. The point is, it's a conversation, and **what's great about conversations is that they're the most natural way that we communicate** as humans. So, generally, that is the easiest stepping stone to getting used to sharing your ideas and perspectives on a regular basis.

The other benefit of this style is that your authority grows based on your association with the people you are interviewing. The more experts and influencers you have conversations with, the more social proof you have of your position and influence in an industry.

The last form, which I recommend the most for people who are looking to demonstrate their expertise is *commentary*. In this format, **you are creating something that is your own**. You look at the world and provide your perspective on a regular basis. It is the most effective way to share your ideas and demonstrate your expertise.

> The only way to have original thoughts is for you to continually present ideas and react and respond to them. And, sometimes, to create your own ideas based on what you've seen in the industry. Every idea today is built on the back of something that came before it. But you can't do that unless you are already learning and participating in the conversation.

Start by bringing all the conversations together. Embed yourself in industry knowledge, then have conversations. Provide your own commentary and perspective based on what you're learning, especially when your audience is behind you in terms of learning those same things. You can be the person that they're following to gain knowledge in their industry.

As you start creating content, there are three things to focus on as you build your personal brand. We'll discuss these in full detail in the next few chapters:

- Your heroic evergreen platform

- Consistent direct communication with your audience

- Scaling your effort and visibility

Chapter Six

Build Your Heroic Evergreen Platform

Your heroic evergreen platform is a virtual or physical place that connects your ideas to the rest of the world. Your content needs a place to live and breathe. That place becomes a part of your brand image and identity. You design it, build it, and grow it, and eventually it takes on a life of its own.

What Is a Platform?

A platform is an organized container for all your ideas, commentary, and conversation. The key is that it is organized. Your platform must be something that allows people to find your content easily. This is a place where you'll continue to deposit new pieces of content on a regular basis. And that content needs to be categorized, searchable, and findable by your audience.

Typically, your platform lives on an online media channel that is organized for long-form content. Standard media channels include things like blog websites, podcasts, video channels, and content pages on your website. Your platform can also be offline in the form of books, newsletters, recurring events, speeches, or workshops. But let's focus on the digital formats for now.

One primary media channel is enough to get you started. But the long-term goal is to establish your platform across the media channels where your audience consumes content.

Why Do Platforms Matter?

Having your platform across these different popular media channels allows people to find you in the formats where they consume content the most. The more places you can put your platform, the more discoverable your platform will be.

What's great about a platform living on a media channel is that once it's created, it exists forever. From the day it's created, it starts to accumulate and grow every week. You can add new pieces of content to your platform any time you want. And if you do that every week, at the end of a year, you'll have a fifty-two-episode platform with real depth.

For your audience's ease of use, your media channels can be organized to share highlights and category ideas, and to gather themes of content. They can be set up as an episodic list, running from beginning to end. Or they can be set up to share new content every week so that your audience can find your newest and greatest materials. The best thing about a media channel is that it is organized by you.

It takes a little time to understand the media channels that your platform can live on. Take time to understand how your audience uses each channel, and then structure and organize your content within those channels to serve that audience.

Once you've built a platform on a media channel that you are happy with, one that's big enough to hold all your ideas, it can be used as a tool for your audience, network, and influence development.

Your platform is typically formatted as a show. That show has an identity, voice, purpose, and specific themes that cater to an audience. Once you have that show, you can reach out to people and invite them into your world.

As soon as the name of your show exists, you can tell people that you have a show and invite them to listen, watch, read, or participate. Tell everyone you know what the show is about and the ideas you want to share. As you invite people to come on the show to discuss their ideas with you, this show becomes its own machine for idea generation and sharing.

The Power of Evergreen Content

Creating and posting evergreen content is one of the secrets to longevity. In content creation, evergreen content makes sense today and in the future. It does not expire.

Evergreen content talks about universal ideas and truths that will remain consistently relevant now and into the future. Once it's created, it becomes its own asset that grows and thrives. The benefit you derive from it right now will also grow and continue.

Evergreen content is a compounding marketing asset that drives attention and grows. For example, if you create one show that talks about a specific idea and that content becomes popular on a media channel like YouTube, or on other social media channels, it can build an audience for you. If people search for that episode on those channels, you can be shown to those audiences over and over again, as long as the content is relevant and findable.

If it's a popular piece of content, it may stay at the top of search results far into the future. You can update evergreen content to keep it relevant, especially the pieces that have proven to be popular.

The opposite of evergreen content is one-off content. This is something that is topical or trending now but which may not be relevant tomorrow. One-off content creates one-time attention. One-time attention from content can be huge, but it can also be fleeting. Any one-off content you create and post typically disappears the day after you share it.

There is value to both types of content. One-off content is great at getting you discovered, but it can take a lot of effort without guaranteeing a reward. The goal is to create things that continue to deliver value to you and your audience over and over again, in the long term.

Heroic Content to the Rescue

To be a thought leader with your content, you must make it heroic. Heroic content is content that leads the way. Sharing a perspective that positions you as a thought leader in your industry allows you to be found and noticed. Your goal is to have a heroic, bold perspective within your category of expertise that shares a useful opinion, letting people know your perspective in your category of information.

That **heroic, bold perspective stands out because it is unique to you**. It is your opinion on something relevant in your industry. The great thing about opinions is that they come from you—from your experience, history, ideas, feelings, and thoughts. Your opinions, the reasons your opinions exist, and the history behind those opinions are unique to you.

You may have opinions that people agree or disagree with, and that is the power of opinions. When you create an opinion and you share it as a heroic perspective, it creates a point where the audience must decide whether they agree with you or disagree with you. In that agreement and disagreement, you find connection and conversation that attracts attention from your audience.

A heroic perspective may not be easy to create, but it is powerful when you figure out how to do it consistently. To create a bold perspective, start with a topic and figure out what part of the conversation you want to participate in. Then choose what matters in that conversation and what your opinion is about it. For example, most content starts with a problem that you are dealing with.

Every person has something preventing them from succeeding in their goals. Your job is to come up with what the list of solutions are in your industry and then decide what matters. You get to decide what is important to you in terms of success for others based on your perspective in an industry.

It will only work when you have a level of expertise, experience, or exposure to speak from. The goal is to tell your audience what to focus on within the problem that they need solved. Share your opinion and what seems to matter most. There are a lot of factors involved in every decision, but usually there's a level of priority set to specific topics within those issues, and you get to decide what your opinion is of what matters most.

An easy exercise to turn this idea into reality would be to pick a topic that people are struggling with in your industry. Look at the solutions, and then create a statement that shares your most simple point of view on the one solution that you think matters most. Then tell people what you believe is the best solution.

That statement should say, "I believe that this one thing is the only thing that matters in finding success with this problem," and then fill in the blanks, explaining your reasoning.

In your development of that belief, you'll start to form stories around your experience that informed that opinion. Your audience gets to agree or disagree with your bold opinion.

The power of a heroic perspective is that it is bold. A lot of people do not break through because they sound like everyone else. They do not dare to be bold and share an opinion because it is not a fact, but facts do not elicit conversations; bold opinions do.

Facts are just information, but opinions inspire ideas. The best content, that which positions you as a thought leader in your industry, must be bold and deliver an original opinion around a specific topic.

If you are out there creating content, start to separate yourself from the competition and ignite your creativity. Build something that has those key components combined:

- Heroic – A bold perspective that positions you as a thought leader in your industry

- Evergreen – A universal idea or truth that remains relevant now and into the future

- Platform – A container for your ideas that has compounding content that is organized, searchable, and findable

Once you create your heroic evergreen platform, you now have a home base and a starting point for the rest of your journey as a personal brand and thought leader.

Activity Break: Set Up Your Platforms

Get started setting up your platforms. Here are a few places to start. These worksheets are available at BrandonBirkmeyer.com/FCL.

Social Media Platforms

- Choose a consistent and professional photo and background for your social media profiles. Make sure the profile photo and account are visible to the public.

- Create a profile description that explains the industry you work in, who you help, and how you help.

- Leverage the contact link in your profile to send people to a curated list of links (not your website). I like to aggregate my resource links on a single landing page or on a link sharing tool like Linktree. Include links to your helpful resources as well as a link to contact you, a link to see your best content, and a link to subscribe to your channels.

Blogging Platforms

- Set up your home for blogging on your own website or on a free site like Medium, Substack, or LinkedIn Articles.

- Write a brief summary about yourself and your content on the "about" page or in the profile description.

- Add a photo to your author profile (the same photo you use consistently on your social media profiles).

Video Platforms

- Set up a YouTube page for any future video content. Choose a name for the page.

- Add your page description, a profile photo, and a background photo.

- Create a playlist for videos that you create.

- Create a playlist for videos that feature you (that other people created) that you can reshare. This may include shows on which you were a guest or any collaborations with other video creators.

- Choose a video to set as the feature video on your YouTube main page. This can be a trailer or feature of your best content, or it could be a video of you describing your YouTube channel.

Audio Platforms

- Set up a playlist on your YouTube channel for any audio content, such as podcast interviews.

- Open a free podcasting account on Spotify to create your own audio content or to create and share interviews as a podcast.

- Pick a podcast name, upload cover art for the podcast, choose your podcast topic category, and write a description of the show.

Interview with Nicky Saunders
IG: @THISISNICKYS

Nicky Saunders and Mostafa Ghonim are the hosts of *Nicky and Moose the Podcast*, a show that takes an inside look at some of the world's top personal brands and businesses to reveal the blueprint behind their success. The show began as a weekly series on Facebook Live, eventually branching out to other media channels, and is now one of my favorite video podcasts on YouTube.

I had a chance to interview Nicky Saunders about the launch and evolution of the show. Nicky is a content creator and keynote speaker in the personal branding and social media industry. She began as a strategist working to grow the online community of Eric Thomas, a very popular motivational speaker. She helped increase his Facebook and Instagram accounts from three hundred thousand to two million followers in a year and a half. Today, Nicky runs a digital marketing agency, coaches, offers digital courses, and runs an online membership community called Deeper Than the Brand.

How to Come up with the Idea for a Show

Brandon Birkmeyer: I'd love to hear what the idea for the original show was and how you got it going.

Nicky Saunders: I am a low-key/high-key nerd, meaning I will watch interviews, read, and listen to audiobooks during the majority of my day and take notes. I have a best friend named Moose who I would bounce different ideas, quotes, and lessons off, and he would always spin it from a business perspective.

I was always looking at the branding and marketing side of things. It started in the pandemic when they released that Michael Jordan documentary, *The Last Dance*. We broke down the documentary through Facebook Live, looking at the branding and business lessons we could learn from the Chicago Bulls basketball team.

We didn't think about it as a podcast yet. My goal was to see if it was valuable content—enough to build an audience. I used Facebook Live because it was the platform that I had at the time. It was the easiest to use for showing video clips while live. We would show video clips first and then go into our discussion. It did so well that we did it twice a week for about three months, and then we looked at creating a podcast.

We took a week off from the live and concentrated on our first podcast episode, which was about Floyd Mayweather, the pro boxer. I still hate that episode to this day because every tech issue went wrong. We rerecorded it about five times. Your first one is never going to be the greatest, but you must put it out there.

How to Choose What Media Channels to Focus On

Brandon Birkmeyer: Do you consider your show a podcast, a YouTube channel, or something else?

Nicky Saunders: I'm just creating it as a show, but I'm mindful of how people consume content. We invested in the microphones the second we turned it into a podcast. When we started getting serious with YouTube, we got the right camera and the right equipment. This is bigger than just audio—bigger than just video. It can be consumed in multiple ways. It's a super educational show that is the blueprint to how this person did it.

Brandon Birkmeyer: How do you think about the different media channels when you're creating content?

Nicky Saunders: I use social media as a tool to become a global brand. I think about how we are strategically taking our viewers through the journey.

I've got to give them little bite-size clips because they don't know me. The clips give some type of functional value, such as tips, tricks, and "how to" content.

Then they go to YouTube, or the podcast, and they get the longer form content. If they like it, they want to know what to do next. So, we have different programs they can join and learn from.

We, as viewers and creators, are normally attracted to one platform. We may go to multiple ones, but we are always going to prefer one or two. So, concentrate on one and repurpose it for the other. Utilize social media channels to take them through the journey that you want them to take.

How to Come up with Great Topics for Each Episode

Brandon Birkmeyer: On your show, you talk about the news, celebrity stories, and trends in culture. What is your selection process? How are you finding things to talk about that inspire you?

Nicky Saunders: I have two processes. I have what people are talking about and then what is a deep lesson for me. And, of course, there's a strategy behind it.

If I talk about something that everybody's talking about, that's going to bring more eyes to what I'm doing. But I'm also being very true to the beliefs and values of the brand. I'll never go too controversial.

Then I'm choosing to talk about content I like. What I like is still going to add value to the people and I can be consistent.

We have different segments. We have the *What's Poppin'?* section for the trending side. It creates engagement with the audience. I pick three topics of *Why is this even happening in the world? What can you live without?* Then I'm going through the blueprint, which includes the lessons that inspired me and Moose to share that with the world.

Then we have a *This or That?* section, which is another lesson based off something that we saw from an article or an interview. Here we're discussing if we have different perspectives on it or not. So, that's how I process things. And then all the leftovers I use for my personal content.

Chapter Seven

Create Direct Communication with Your Audience

One of the biggest mistakes in content creation is relying one hundred percent on social media posts to communicate with your audience. Social media is a channel that you can't control. For example, on Instagram, your posts are typically shown to less than five percent of your followers. That means, if you have one hundred followers, less than five will see your post. What a waste of time and effort!

Social media posts aren't the only way to communicate with your audience on social media. You can **directly communicate with your followers through direct messages**. Unfortunately, the only way to send direct messages to all your followers is one at a time. There are no options on social media to reach all your followers at once other than with paid advertising.

Do I hate social media? No (well, sometimes, but for different reasons). While social media posts are bad at reaching your current audience, it's a great tool for getting discovered by new audiences. The better you get at creating content for each channel, the more chances you have at something reaching larger audiences and potentially going viral.

You can get lucky and gain followers quickly on social media. Once you have followers, the best way to directly communicate with them at scale is to invite them to share their contact information with you.

Grow Your Audience on Land That You Own

My favorite communication channels for reaching my audience are email, text message, and membership groups, where you can consistently deliver messages and invite them to be a part of that. It's up to the audience to decide whether they click to open it or not based on the relevance of the message.

Anytime you're releasing content across social media, mention in that content that you have a way for people to get content from you directly. **The most popular form of direct communication is an email list.** You control your email list, which allows you to send out messages as often as you like, and they are always delivered to the inboxes of your audience.

The power to manage that email list, and even to segment and personalize messages to that list, is only found in these direct communication channels. The way to get people to move from social media to your email list is to give them something in return for signing up. You must decide what your people are looking for and continue to try new incentives to move them from being a viewer on social media to a subscriber on your email list.

Incentives are very common in marketing communications. You'll find many examples of this online. These incentives can include some type of solution to a problem that your audience is facing. Those solutions could come in the form of checklists, step-by-step instructions, shortcuts, downloadable guides, and any useful information that provides a quick win for your audience.

You can get creative with this. Figure out what your audience is interested in right now. Decide how you can provide that to them. Some people go as far as to create contests and deliver actual physical prizes or free services as rewards for people who have subscribed to their email lists. Other people create such an interesting newsletter that they only need to describe the value of the newsletter to get people to subscribe.

Create newsletter content that is unique and exclusive to your email list—that can't be found on your other channels. It must be good enough to motivate them to allow you to communicate with them directly. After they are incentivized to be on your list, it's your job to introduce yourself, welcome them to your world, nurture your relationship with them, and send consistent direct communication that is worth reading.

Nurture Your Audience with Helpful Content

The next step in creating consistent direct communication with an audience is to provide thoughtful content and solutions every time you send a message. **Every message you send to your audience must deliver on the promise that you made as a helpful content creator.**

There needs to be a reason that they open your emails every week. That content should be relevant to the reason your audience subscribed in the first place. Understanding your audience is key.

You can learn a lot from the content you post on social media to inform your direct communication. Look at the popularity of your social media and decide what you should be creating in your direct communication with your audience. The more relevant and engaging your content is to your audience, the more likely it is that they will continue to open it every week and be engaged in your ideas.

If your audience has taken the step to become part of your email list, they trust you to not only provide content but also solutions. Sometimes, those solutions can come in the form of more helpful resources. The more you help your audience move through their day-to-day challenges and solve their problems, the more loyal they will be to you.

Become a Consistent Fan Favorite

One of the key factors often overlooked in direct communication with an audience is consistency. Your audience expects you to deliver on schedule. If they look forward to your communications showing up in a specified timeframe, you better show up consistently. Whether it be daily or weekly, you must deliver on the expectations you set at the beginning.

This means that you must always meet your deadlines. Your audience looks forward to the content that you provide, otherwise they wouldn't have subscribed. So, deliver as promised. The longer you go without communicating with your audience on a regular basis, the more likely it is that they will forget why they subscribed.

The most common timing of direct communication is a weekly message. Weekly is great because every person starts fresh and thinks about their timeframes on a weekly basis. Weekly is an easy format that most people can keep up with and stick to. Start there. If you go longer than a week, people sometimes forget that you are in their inbox.

Some email messages make sense for daily distribution or weekday distribution. Those tend to be shorter, daily, helpful solutions for specific industries. You must decide if your message makes sense on a daily or weekly basis.

There aren't many cases where biweekly or monthly direct communication makes sense. It's too far removed from being a part of your audience's consistent lives.

To get this right every time, think about the audience first and ask yourself how you can deliver consistent direct communication to them. Start with the incentives that move people from viewers to subscribers. Your consistent direct communication with subscribers will be some of the most effective content you create on your thought leader journey.

Activity Break: Set Up Your Email Newsletter

Get started setting up your email newsletter. Here are a few places to start. These worksheets are available at BrandonBirkmeyer.com/FCL.

Creating Your Contacts List

- If this is your first time creating an email list, start by collecting the email addresses you already have. Pull all the email addresses from your phone and from email accounts (like Gmail) and add them to a spreadsheet.

- Then pull any email addresses from your connections on social media sites, like Facebook and LinkedIn, and add them to the spreadsheet.

Setting Up Your Emailing Tool

- Set up a free account with an email management tool like ConvertKit or Mailchimp.

- Upload the email addresses you collected from your spreadsheet into the email management tool.

Inviting Your Contacts to Subscribe to Your List

- Start to draft a new email. In that email, say hello to your contact, let them know you plan to start sharing industry news and perspectives on a particular topic and that you hope you can include them in your friend group that receives those emails. Mention that they can unsubscribe anytime.

- Create a title for your email that says something like "Something new I'm working on" or "How've you been?" Keep it simple, and be authentic.

- Add your contacts to the email and hit send. Note that this only works using an email management tool. Do not send mass emails from a regular email account such as Gmail.

Writing Your Welcome Sequence

- For new people that choose to subscribe to your emails, write an introductory email thanking them for subscribing and telling them a little bit more about you and what they can expect to read in your future emails.

- As you grow, you can create a second and third email to add to the sequence that shares some of your best content and resources or invites them to set up a networking call with you.

- After your welcome emails, the new subscribers will be added to the list of people who receive your regular newsletter emails.

Writing Your First Newsletter

- In the beginning, keep your emails short and personal. You can start by giving a brief update on what you are up to as a little icebreaker. This can be about your professional life or your personal life, but keep it light.

- Then mention any industry news or insights you'd like to share. Or provide a link to an article you've written or content you've created.

- In one of your emails, consider asking your contacts what they are interested in hearing more about. This can help you craft engaging content next time around.

Interview with Kat Norton

IG: @MISS-EXCEL

K at Norton is known online and on social media as Miss Excel. You can find her fun and engaging videos on TikTok where she teaches you how to use Microsoft Excel while dancing and entertaining. Kat was recently awarded the Microsoft MVP Award and was named one of the top influencers of 2021 by *Forbes*. She is effectively leveraging the power of consistent direct communication with her audience.

This is, by far, one of the most entertaining ways I've ever seen someone teach a program like Microsoft Excel. In a short period of time, she leveraged these viral videos to grow her community on TikTok and Instagram to over a million followers each. But it wasn't until she shifted her efforts to growing her email list that she was able to turn that great content into a lead engine for her business.

How to Find Your Content Voice

Brandon Birkmeyer: I'd love to hear how you went from a nine-to-five corporate job to becoming a TikTok creator and entrepreneur.

Kat Norton: I was working at a global consulting firm doing securitization reviews for banks, which is as fun as it sounds. I was also teaching Microsoft Excel internally for the company. I did that for about four and a half years. And then, with the start of the pandemic, I found myself back in my childhood bedroom of my parents' house—twenty-seven years old and trying to figure out what I wanted to do with my life.

I was on the phone with my best friend, spitballing different ideas and side hustles I could do with my Excel skills. She suggested I put my Excel tips on TikTok. I didn't even have the app on my phone, but after she said it, I could not shake this idea.

I made my secret TikTok account, Miss-Excel, and I started posting one video a day. By the fourth video, I was reaching a hundred thousand views of my videos and started getting pushed to all these people. Within about three weeks, I had my first TikTok video go viral and hit three million seven hundred thousand views. I had a hundred thousand followers within a couple of days of that. I was just flying by the seat of my pants. I added an Instagram account as well to hedge my risk of TikTok getting banned. I went viral on TikTok and Instagram pretty much every month after that for the next few months.

How to Shift from Creator to Entrepreneur

Brandon Birkmeyer: At that point in time, did you know how you wanted to make a business out of this? What was going through your mind when you posted that first video on TikTok.

Kat Norton: The first video was like, *I just wanna see what happens.* I realized when I was making the video that I was getting so much creative fulfillment out of it. People started commenting and saying it helped them. I'm like, let's make this thing. I didn't even really think about courses. I had an MBA, but they didn't teach us stuff like that.

At that point, I didn't really understand email lists and all the bits and pieces. I was just having fun.

Brandon Birkmeyer: You mentioned you got someone who asked you to conduct some training for them. What happened after that? What turned this into a real business for you?

Kat Norton: Back in October of 2020, I had a few hundred thousand followers across the platforms but zero products and zero email list.

Starting an Email List

Kat Norton: A business coach reached out to me and said, "Hey, I notice you have a big following over there but no products."

I was like, *touché, I guess people do that out here*. And so, I did the basics. I got Mailchimp and Linktree. I set up a little automation with a freebie and started growing an email list.

At that point, I was learning the value of an email list. The obvious next step seemed to be to build an Excel course. Something fun, cool, creative, and still very me. I took two weeks off from my day job, and I filmed from my living room.

I started selling courses in November of 2020, and then two months later, the passive income that was being brought in from the courses was more than my day job. Miss Excel took me ten hours a week, whereas my day job took me forty hours a week. At that point, I was like, *I really gotta think about priorities*.

In January of 2021, I quit my consulting job and became a full-time entrepreneur. From there, I built nine more courses and scaled them into a multimillion-dollar business. It was just a matter of creating more volume. I kept growing the audience, posting on all the platforms, doing webinars, and that was what really moved the needle for us.

Then I hired a team because I was doing the whole thing myself—even customer service for fifteen thousand students. We've got a small but mighty team, and the business has grown effortlessly from there. It was just a matter of getting the right things in order.

Brandon Birkmeyer: Let's talk about your email list. Did you sit there and write out email sequences with a certain tool, and how did that go?

Kat Norton: I use Flodesk now because I got in at the beta stage for $20 a month, no matter how big my mailing list is. That has been a huge money saver compared to other platforms that would charge thousands a month based on the size of my list. I use that for my freebie sequence, my webinar sign-up, and any course emails sent from within my courses.

I remember the day I set up that automation. It was the best feeling because when I made the first course, the Excel one, I was manually sending each person's welcome email every time I got a sale. And I was like, *all right, there's gotta be a better way to do this.*

Brandon Birkmeyer: You start with content on your social media channels, and then the audience finds you in a video and is pushed to a link in your bio. What happens after that?

Kat Norton: When I was starting out and first selling it, they would get my top thirty-one functions PDF guide and that would start the five-email sequence. On the fourth email, I'd announce the offer, and the fifth email was the last call email. Those were direct sales. I didn't start doing webinars until April of 2021, and that's when we took the business from six to seven figures quickly.

Chapter Eight

Scale Your Effort and Visibility

When you are actively creating content, you start to establish a rhythm for creating, and you get better as you do it. The content you create will get easier for you and grow to be better and more thoughtful. It will start to be clearer and more aligned with who you are and what you want to talk about. As your message starts to crystallize and your expression starts to become more natural, you want to look for ways to share your content with more people.

The secret to driving audience growth is with scaled effort and visibility. **To get your content seen, you can either share it more often or show it to more people.**

> You may not be ready for this step yet. For many people, scaling up doesn't begin until after a few years of consistent content creation. Some people may never want or need to scale to accomplish their personal goals. Save this step for when you are ready to invest more time, effort, or money into growing beyond your current capabilities.

Showing your content to more people requires paying for advertising and promotion. Or you can share it more often by building systems that help you create more efficiently to increase your volume. High-volume content is content that can be produced at a high rate of creation and distribution. Most active creators have a schedule that creates one piece of long-form content or a few different pieces of short-form content per week. But how do you go from creating once per week to creating a few times per day?

The goal of creating enough content every day is that you have more chances to be seen on a regular basis by your audience. High-volume content is typically rewarded by most media channels with added reach to new audiences. The more you create, the more people will see your content.

The problem is that creating content at a high volume takes a lot of work and effort. That effort can come in the creation of the content or the production and distribution of the content.

Beyond that, the content that you want to create more often must also be more creative. So now we're looking at more to do and we must be more thoughtful about it. Being more creative means that it must better capture the attention of the audiences that we are serving.

You can start by covering topics that are more interesting and topical. Look for content ideas that have stronger interest and that would be more engaging to watch. Do your research into what's trending, and be more strategic about how you hook people in to watch. Find ways to grab attention immediately, right at the beginning of the content. Leverage the titles and visual creative that is shown to your audience in the first place.

Scaling your content production is not easy work. This is something that takes place at a more advanced level of content creation. The reason it takes place later is because it takes a lot more resources, time, and money to achieve these types of results.

Beyond being high volume and more creative, it also must be more expressive. It should tap into more beliefs that come from you that are original in a way that is very natural.

Find What Works Best for You

So, how do you find a way to express yourself more naturally and more often?

Start by finding the form of expression that works best for you as a creator. It's your job to figure out where you are most comfortable creating. That's going to involve things like figuring out the time of day that you create best or the circumstances in which you create best based on the environment or behavior around you. It involves finding places that inspire you and which are easy for you to create in.

Find a place to create with very few barriers to you starting that creation process. You want to pick a place where all you need to do is push a button and start. Also, **create an environment where you are feeling creative**. That might include a certain type of day or a certain activity that gets you into the mindset where you're excited and motivated to create.

Content is now your job. You must determine what work cadence will get the most out of you. For some, it will mean one day per week is dedicated to content creation and all they do is create back-to-back. For others, it might be aligned with certain feelings, working only when they're feeling creative.

Either way, you must design an environment that allows you to express yourself more often. This might also mean figuring out how to get other things off your plate so you can focus on the creative instead of the operations of your business.

This is the stage, for content creators, where we're thinking about leveling up. That means doing what you do best while allowing other people to take on jobs that you either don't do well or don't want to do; in other words, delegating. Start with figuring out where you can create most naturally, most often, and lean into that, making that space your own.

Once you have a system for constantly expressing yourself in the most natural way, you must find a way to put that content in as many places as possible.

Leverage Your Content with Intentional Repurposing

Intentional repurposing occurs when you remake and reformat your content for multiple media channels. **Your content is a product that can be repurposed across multiple formats and channels.**

One long-form video can be converted into short-form videos via social media clips. It can also be converted into an audio format for a podcast or an edited video format for a YouTube channel.

That long-form content can also be converted into text format for a blog. And you can add images and videos to a blog post to make it more engaging.

The secret is that the creative cannot simply be put on every channel as is. It must first be repurposed creatively to best suit the channels and their formats. An audience watching a YouTube video expects very different things than an audience listening to a podcast or an audience reading a blog post.

Wherever you create first, whether it's a video podcast, a live stream, a YouTube video, or a blog post, **your priority as you scale is to figure out how to repurpose**. For example, with a channel like YouTube, the visual video element must be very engaging.

- Include a strong hook at the beginning.

- Use great editing to cut out all the fluff that the audience doesn't need.

- Raise the energy high enough to keep the audience listening and paying attention for the whole video.

- Shorten the content from what was initially recorded to only show what's relevant for that video.

You get to choose the mode of creation; it's up to you to **find your most natural way of expressing yourself**. But the next step is always going to be figuring out how to best adapt how you create into the format your audience consumes.

People don't consume and engage with content the same way across every channel. Be intentional about the outcome of your repurposing. Make your content effective on all channels. Otherwise, you're just spraying content across channels, and it will be ignored.

Create Efficient Systems for Production and Distribution

The last barrier to overcome when building scale and visibility as a content creator is to create low-involvement, high-volume production and distribution systems.

Systems make content production at scale possible. A system allows you to do something in an organized way that repeats itself. Your system will reduce your effort as a creator. This **non-creative effort needs to be low involvement and high volume**. The system will always have inputs and it's up to you to determine what inputs are yours versus what steps are to be taken by either other people on your team or other tools that can automate your process. A lot of the time spent in content creation for a content creator is on the production side. Taking what you make and turning it into other things takes time.

Every channel has a different level of editing needs, but they all require effort. Whether it's video editing, sound editing, color editing, or text editing, there's always something that needs to be adjusted to make it serve the audience better. Finding ways to create a process for that is highly important when you're looking to scale.

If you were to edit a one-hour video, it would take you a couple of hours or more. That editing time limits you from doing more creating and is not the best use of your time. Being a great creator doesn't mean you are a great editor.

A big step in the process of creating more content at a higher volume is to find people and tools that can handle those tasks for you. Content production is one of the heavier parts of scaling your system, but there are great tools and great freelancers for outsourcing that are accessible today for creators.

The trick is to find your system for doing that. Your system will typically involve figuring out your own steps, finding things you can outsource to other people, and leveraging technology to automate manual processes.

After you figure out your systems and processes for producing a lot of content, move on to distribution. You must distribute this content across all the media channels. Unfortunately, **you can't just repost your content everywhere**. Every post requires inputs, including uploading the videos and images, adding text to describe those images, and filling in other areas of a form or format that are required by each media channel.

For social media, it's usually just text and tagging. For long-form channels, it can involve things like cover art, descriptions, titles, episode numbers, and categorization.

This type of work that helps distribute your content is easier when you only have one episode per week. But when you scale that to three times per day or more, the distribution time skyrockets.

Establish your system for getting these things posted on the correct platforms. You can use tools that automate scheduling posts. There are virtual assistants who can help you with some of the work. There are social media planners who can manage your channels. Some of the things you can do yourself.

All these factors and choices go into building your system. It can take time to build it all out, but it's necessary if you are looking to scale up.

> Creating systems that work for all channels and formats can be overwhelming. A good starting point is to find a couple of tools for content creation, content editing, and content distribution that you know how to use. If you don't know how to use one, learn how to use one for each channel.

Find out what tools are best for your needs by testing several of them. Once you've found the right ones, figure out your system for using them so that you can show someone else. I find that you will need one tool to edit your content, one tool to transcribe your content, and one tool to convert your content from long form to short form.

When you're starting, you can consider using one virtual assistant. You can walk them through the steps of the process so they can do each of the needed tasks for you using the tools that you selected.

The most important skill for a virtual assistant is the ability to edit text accurately. Most people can learn how to post on social media, but it takes natural skill to understand how to edit text and find the right clips that create impact for your audience.

If you are a heavy video creator that leverages YouTube, you will also want to find a professional video editor, whose top skill is editing for YouTube.

You can try these things yourself to experiment and find what works for you along the way. The system is not easy to build, but once it's built, you will unlock the opportunity for massive attention.

Activity Break: Set Up Your Content Plan

Get started setting up your content plan. Here are a few places to start. These worksheets are available at BrandonBirkmeyer.com/FCL.

Picking Topics

- Select one broad topic and three subtopics to focus on.

- Select at least three industry news sources that you will follow to stay informed and to inspire content ideas.

- Enter your topics and content ideas into a brainstorming tool like AnswerThePublic to see what questions are being asked about the topic that you can respond to.

Scheduling Time for Content

- Determine your planned content release day (Monday to Sunday) and schedule it daily, weekly, or monthly. Create a calendar of ideas.

- Block out time in your schedule for content creation; either in small blocks each week or bigger blocks of time less frequently (to batch multiple pieces of content at once).

Posting Content

- Pick at least one primary content channel or social media channel to start posting content on. Add in channels as you get more proficient or have more time. Post consistently.

Formats

- Choose the size and shape of your posts (i.e., square, portrait, landscape), the length of your videos (i.e., fifteen, thirty, or sixty seconds; two minutes to sixty minutes), or the word count of your posts and articles (i.e., fifty to two-hundred-word posts, eight hundred to twelve-hundred-word articles, or three-thousand-plus-word blog posts).

- Adapt your content to the best practices of each channel you post on.

Systems

- Write down the steps you take each week and use that to create a checklist that you can consistently follow.

- Pick what tools you will use to support recurring tasks such as graphic design, text editing, transcription, audio/video editing, captioning, and social media scheduling.

- If you have a content budget, decide what tools you will subscribe to, what work you will outsource, and what content you will sponsor or support with advertising.

Interview with Roberto Blake

IG: @ROBERTOBLAKE

R oberto Blake is a creative entrepreneur, keynote speaker, and podcaster who hosts a YouTube channel that has over five hundred thousand subscribers and thirty-five million views. He's the author of the book, *Create Something Awesome*, he's been listed in *Forbes' 20 Must Watch YouTube Channels That Will Change Your Business*, and he leverages prolific creative expression through YouTube.

Roberto is one of today's leading experts on the creator economy and is the founder of the Awesome Creator Academy, which coaches creators on how to build a full-time income. He's published over fifteen hundred videos on his main YouTube channel and has helped thousands of content creators go full-time. He has participated in over two thousand live streams in eight years across multiple platforms and publicly responds to hundreds of questions weekly on social media from content creators and online business owners.

Unlocking Your Creative Expression

Brandon Birkmeyer: What is the mindset that people need to have going into this creator mode?

Roberto Blake: The hardest thing for most people is to sit still and do something for ninety minutes at a time. That's peak productivity. Then, you have to be able to sit and watch a tutorial that might be twenty or thirty minutes, then spend the next hour executing what you learned.

People don't have the ability to do that day in and day out for a year. It takes ten thousand hours to master a new skill, but a hundred hours is competency. If you don't believe me, look up how many hours you must log to be able to drive a car. Look at how many hours you need to drive a commercial truck. You only need a hundred and fifty flight hours to be a certified pilot.

Most people won't even put in a hundred hours to learn the primary skill sets of a content creator. Whether they're a YouTuber or podcaster, they will not put a hundred hours into each of the primary skills needed, whether that's video editing or audio editing, production, learning cameras or microphones, lighting, hardware, etc.

They won't put a hundred hours into learning SEO, or copywriting, or social media marketing, but then they'll be surprised when they fail. Maybe you spent ten hours learning, but did you spend a hundred hours practicing the ten? If the answer is no, I'm not shocked that you don't have results—you are not upholding your end of the bargain.

At your nine-to-five job, you work forty hours a week to produce a result for an employer, and then you're shocked when your four or five hours a week of effort don't give you a replaceable income. Think of all the education used to train you for the job that you currently have, or the job you spent four years in school getting a degree to qualify for. Really? Really?

You need realism, and you need the time freedom of fifteen to twenty-five hours of productive work. It takes that long to start accomplishing something. You'd still have to do that for one to three years to see some real results. By real results, I mean maybe getting monetized on YouTube, maybe, through multiple revenue streams, making $1,000 to $2,000 a month, which may not replace your full-time income.

Redeploy this capital into building an asset, such as building your own independent media company that's going to produce intellectual property you will benefit from in perpetuity. That's a different mindset shift as well. The mindset shift from worker and employee to creative entrepreneur is huge.

Leveraging Content at Scale as a Prolific Creator

Brandon Birkmeyer: How do you approach audience growth as a content creator?

Roberto Blake: Audience growth is about the combination of reach, reputation, and relationships. I'm also a big anime nerd, and one of my favorite anime is called Naruto. It's about ninjas who use superpowers. And there's this superpower they use called the clone technique where you can make physical copies of yourself that can do what you do.

Imagine making twenty clones of yourself. You could make them do all your work and your studying, and all of the knowledge and everything that they learn will come to you as the original. You have clones that study all day and learn for you, clones that go into the world to make you money, clones to go to all the networking events, and a clone that answers your direct messages. They'd do everything for you.

Okay, so here's the thing. Content is cloning. Content is cloning.

When I make content, I clone myself. Every time I make a piece of content, every time I make a video, it goes out there as a foot soldier in my army, making me money. Because it's monetized, a video that I make is a clone of Roberto Blake going out and getting me money. My content represents me in the world and it's building new relationships. It's increasing my reach and building my reputation. My content is providing me with analytics data about my audience.

Content serves as our clones. I have thousands of pieces of content—thousands of clones that work for me twenty-four seven. They do not need to eat or sleep, will not call in sick, and will not ask me for a raise. My clone army is out in the world building new relationships for me on a regular basis, scaling my reputation, allowing me to be reachable in new ways, and generating revenue for me.

Listen to the full interviews at BrandonBirkmeyer.com/FCL.

Building Community

A personal brand is just as much about the community of people around you as it is about who you are and what you put out into the world.

When someone starts to build a personal brand and create content, they think of their community as the audience that will find them through their content and online presence. But it's more than that.

For a personal brand, community starts with the people you already know and the places you frequently go.

As a new content creator building a personal brand, an easy trap to fall into is to focus on posting content online and hoping that the algorithms of the various social media channels will send you an audience.

It's not easy to build an audience on social media. It takes time, knowledge, and a little bit of luck. Luck is not a strategy, and you don't have any time to waste.

The real audience building strategy to use when you are getting started is networking, partnering, and speaking. The reality is that audience building for new leaders requires more of your personal time and effort—getting in front of people, doing outreach, and making yourself known to the communities and industries that matter to you.

Think about where you can show up to meet new people. In the beginning, you are not the center of your community. You are one part of an existing ecosystem. The community that you eventually build doesn't start around you; it starts where people are already gathering.

Your job is to participate in those existing communities that align with who you are and how you help. When you participate, the goal is to build relationships and add value to other people. As you nurture those relationships, you develop influence with those people. Think about how you can add value, be of service, participate, and develop influence with as many relevant people as possible.

> You may have to explore many different types of communities in the beginning. There are a lot of existing communities out there, and the only way to know if they are a good fit is to join them and participate. For example, you can join your local BNI (business networking international) group specifically built for local word-of-mouth referrals. You can join a coworking space in your local city to meet other entrepreneurs and business owners, or your chamber of commerce to meet founders of local businesses. Do whatever you can to meet more people.

Your goal is to show up in as many places as possible with other people so you can tell them who you are, what you do (not to sell to them), and get to know them. Then follow up with the people you meet to set up a future chat to deepen the relationship further. After you meet people, find ways to get to know more about what they do, especially if you meet people that would potentially be good for your service.

If nothing else, seek out people who have great energy and could connect you to potential clients. You can always **spot the person in the room who tends to know a lot of people**. Introduce yourself to the event host or find the outgoing person introducing other people. Find that person who always has people around them. Get out into different communities and meet as many people as possible.

You can be selective with the events that make most sense for you. Personally, I was slow to meet people locally. I was more interested in going to industry conferences that were a little farther away. I was going to marketing conferences, social media summits, podcasting expos and entrepreneurial events. That's where I was most comfortable meeting people in the beginning.

As you participate in more places and meet more people, they start to get to know and recognize you. As those relationships develop over time, those people start to become your supporters and your community. That's when you need to represent yourself, let them know what you do, and follow up. Just showing up isn't enough.

Develop the habit of going to events on a regular basis, introducing yourself, following up, and nurturing relationships. Get to know people and set up one-on-one conversations. After each event you attend, make a list of people that you can connect with. You are not reaching out to offer services yet, just getting to know people better. Be genuinely interested in what they do, get to know their pain points, and listen for ways you can add value.

The help you offer doesn't have to be your own service or business. You can be helpful by making introductions and providing referrals, listening and being someone for them to talk to, or by sending them something thoughtful like an article or book recommendation based on a relevant conversation you had with them. You could even take the extra step and purchase a book for them.

The more you put yourself out there and participate in communities, **focusing your energy outwards instead of inwards**, the better off you will be.

There are three things to focus on when building a community for a personal brand:

- Purposeful places to participate

- Influential industry relationships

- High-profile engagements

The more effort you put into developing these three key areas, the better you will be at building your personal brand.

Chapter Nine

Seek Out Purposeful Places to Participate

There are already people you know—in your industry, your business, and your life—who can help you on your journey. As you decide to grow, you can seek out new places and create new connections. This is especially true for those people who haven't done a great job of building industry relationships to begin with, and we've all been guilty of that.

However, there are always more events you could have gone to, more networking opportunities that you could have taken advantage of, and more times you could have put yourself out there to volunteer and be a part of something in your industry that was bigger than you or your company. As you are building your personal brand, it's up to you to seek out purposeful places to participate—and the first place to look are places that are aligned with industries you serve.

Places Aligned with Industries You Serve

Sometimes, your expertise is in one industry but your clients are in a different industry. For example, if you are an accountant, you are in the accounting industry. But your customers may be in a different industry—the entertainment, financial, health, or any other industry.

To meet the people who need to hear your message and who may want to build a relationship with you, you must seek out people in an industry that you serve. Yes, sometimes you serve multiple industries. Pick one or two priority industries to engage with.

Find an event to attend from a top association in your chosen industry. Find a local business group or networking group. Do your research and figure out where the people you serve come together, and then find a way to participate. **Participation means joining the organization or the event, showing up in person, and starting to get to know the people in the organization.**

> When you go to these industry places, the goal is not to sell. The goal is to build relationships and add value. Find places where you can participate. Engage with the community of people, and add value in any way you can, based on the skills you have.

Many times, when you're starting new relationships, the only and best way you can serve is by listening to your community of people and offering introductions to other people that you know. Potentially, after speaking with someone, you can send resources or reference material that addresses the problem they brought up in your conversation.

The simplest way you can participate is by showing up consistently and being active and engaged in the community. When the community is doing something, **be the person that shows up every time**. Raise your hand, volunteer, and communicate often and enthusiastically.

Places Connected to Your Area of Expertise

You don't want to forget about places connected to your specific area of expertise. If you are in a specific industry, there are lots of people who do the same thing you do. Though you may view them as competition, the truth is that there's a lot to be gained from building relationships with people who have similar experiences and expertise as yourself.

Even at the very beginning, having someone to talk to that's struggling with the same issues you're facing will help you feel more connected and less alone on your journey to building your personal brand. The added benefit of getting to know more people who are similar in terms of expertise is that you get to share ideas about common trends and topics in your industry.

Simply having regular conversations with people in your industry leaves you better informed and therefore a better expert in your industry. **The best ideas come in conversation rather than in isolation.**

Oftentimes, those relationships with people who you see as competition can lead to unforeseen benefits and advantages for you in the future. Whether that be a referral from someone who does what you do, that they don't want or need, or through recommendations for potential opportunities through their relationships.

The more people you know, the better chance you have of being found through their connections and their communities. The best people to get to know in your area of expertise tend to be leaders in your industry. So, don't just get to know anyone in your industry; get to know those who are writing books, speaking on topics, and who are influencing your industry.

Many times, an event has speakers in your industry that you can show up and introduce yourself to. Typically, industry speakers are accessible because they are not celebrities. They are generally happy to have conversations with other people in their industry, especially those who are also trying to make a name for themselves to become thought leaders.

Make a list of the places, events, groups, and communities in your industry, then go out and find those industry leaders. You can start with a hundred people that you'd love to meet and then figure out how you can cross paths with some of those people more often. See if they have their own communities, their own networks, or if they're showing up to places where you can go.

If you're already creating content, you can invite those people to participate in your content and potentially be a guest on your show. Maybe they will reciprocate, and you can go on their show as well. Or become a part of their community, and gain additional community exposure through the people you meet.

Places Inspired by Your Personal Growth Goals

Other places you can look to grow your community are places driven by your own interests and curiosity. Participate in places inspired by your personal growth goals.

You are on your own journey of self-development, and on that journey, you will find specific skills that you want to learn or programs that you want to join. **Make a list of the skills that you want to develop and your personal growth goals and chase them.**

Don't just read books and do research online. The places where you can go to learn and develop the critical skills you're inspired to learn often provide opportunities for you to build community. People who are on the same learning journey as you may have a lot in common with you, and as you grow at the same pace that they grow, they can become allies in your future development. Even if they are in a different industry than you, those relationships can turn into great referral partnerships.

When you participate in these communities, make sure that you **show up and seek out people to share the journey with.** When you are in those places of personal growth, take the extra step to reach out to the other people in the group and invite them into a relationship with you.

Activity Break: Set Up Your Networking Plan

Get started setting up your networking plan. Here are a few places to start. These worksheets are available at BrandonBirkmeyer.com/FCL.

Managing Your Calendar

- Make a list of events and meetups that you are interested in attending over the next twelve months. Add them to your calendar.

- Pick your top three to five events or meetups. Commit to going or RSVP and get tickets. Mark them on your calendar as "busy."

Networking Plan

- Before the event, see if you know anyone going, or reach out and get someone to go with you. At the very least, get familiar with the event team, event host, or leadership team of the group.

- Review the event agenda and attendees. Connect with a handful of speakers and attendees before the event. Follow their social media and send messages to anyone you find interesting to introduce yourself.

- Set up meetings or join meetups associated with the event ahead of time.

Relationship Building

- Determine what your icebreaker topics are for the event. Usually, it's related to the topic/theme of the event. Think about what you have in common with people attending the event and lead with that.

- Plan out how you will introduce yourself at the event. Decide what is relevant about you to them that you want to share, and what you will ask them to get to know them better.

- At the event, put yourself in places where people congregate such as near the entrances, in the food/drink lines, or at the tables/chairs. Say hello to the people around you. Make sure to request to connect online or via email with the people you meet.

Follow Up

- After the event, make a list of everyone you met, where you met them, and what you spoke about.

- Reach out to everyone you met, tell them what you enjoyed about meeting them, and invite them to a follow-up chat to continue the conversation.

- On the follow-up call, do not sell anything. Just get to know the other person and their career or business. Ask them about what they are working on and about the future. Offer to provide any helpful ideas, resources, or introductions that seem relevant. Be helpful. Plan to check back within three to six months.

Interview with Jay Clouse

IG: @JAYCLOUSE

Jay Clouse began his community-building journey in 2012 when he organized his first Startup Weekend and then about a dozen more events before he began building his first online community, Unreal Collective. That community was acquired by Pat Flynn at SPI Media in 2020. For the following year, Jay led the community experience team at SPI, developing their membership community, course community, and cohort-based courses.

Jay's podcast, *Creator Science*, has generated more than two million downloads in two years. He has grown an email list to over thirty-three thousand subscribers, developed eleven online courses, and generated over $150,000 in digital product sales in two years.

Community Growth Through One-on-One Outreach

Brandon Birkmeyer: How did you start building attention for your community and coaching business?

Jay Clouse: I started writing every day, and that was what I was really interested in, but I still needed to make money, and I was self-employed. So, I offered services.

I was offering a facilitated mastermind service where I'd work with fifteen to twenty people at a time. And I was doing some one-on-one coaching on top of that. My selling was one-to-one.

I was creating content, and I would talk about the opportunity to work with me in that content. But I couldn't count on that to convert fifteen to twenty people every twelve weeks. My audience just wasn't that big.

In my day-to-day life, I was meeting with people one-on-one constantly. If they talked about something that made me think they might be a fit for that program, I'd take note. Then, when it came time for enrollment, which would only happen two or three times per year, I would reach out to them directly.

If it became obvious on the phone call that they needed me, meaning I could look them in the eyes and say, "This will help you, and you'll be glad you did it," I'd win the sale.

For a long time, my actual business was supported solely by one-to-one outreach. I was creating content at the same time and, thankfully, the work was good enough that people liked it. They talked about it. They stayed. They started to appreciate my viewpoint on things.

Building Trust with Your Community

Brandon Birkmeyer: What I want to jump into is this idea of the community that's been following you and growing along the way. Do you have a perspective on the right way to bring a community along on your personal brand journey?

Jay Clouse: I think anyone who's following your work is going to naturally be invested in you and your journey. I do think you have to earn people's interest before you talk a lot about yourself.

Tell them something that's useful and relevant and over time, after a period of weeks, months, or years, they're going to be more interested in you because you've become a part of their world. You'll naturally have built a community, following you along in that way, but you must earn that with time.

And even after you earn it, you need to still honor that relationship and not make everything about you. You need to give first. I still have to remind myself that all the time because there are little traps. For example, I'll share something about what I'm working on or what's happening in my life, and I'll get a lot of really positive feedback. And I'll think, *man, I should just talk about that more.*

But it's like a bank. You need to make deposits in the beginning. Then you can take withdrawals on that goodwill.

Brandon Birkmeyer: You take a very friendly approach to talking to people and facilitating conversation in your community. It seems to come naturally to you. Is that something that you've developed over time?

Jay Clouse: Yeah, I think so. I've done a fair amount of public speaking at this point and a fair amount of facilitation. I've learned a lot about myself, frankly. There was a time when I was doing more coaching, but I struggled with the coaching relationship where someone who is paying me to coach them is "othering" me in some way.

They're saying, "You are something that I want to be," or, "You know something that I want to know."

I have this inclination to smash that gap and say, "I'm not up there. I'm just beside you. Actually, we are the same person. We have the same abilities and skills. You just need to think about this differently."

If you remove that aspect of "othering," your words carry less weight. To do them a service, you need to allow yourself to be put on the pedestal that they're putting you on. It became uncomfortable for me to live there. And that's why I don't do it.

Brandon Birkmeyer: There's a responsibility there to them. But then they need to take responsibility for themselves. They can take in your perspective, but it's still on them to make it work.

Jay Clouse: That's also challenging because, ultimately, I can't do the work for you, and I can't convince you to care about something you don't care about. When it comes to the dynamics of speaking with people and helping them out, I very aggressively step out of the coach seat and say, "I'll give my thoughts, but I'm one data point, and I have my own biases and blind spots, and here's where this is coming from."

I think people appreciate that because the Internet has evolved to a point where we recognize tactics. We recognize guru-ism, and we just don't want it. I don't want to participate in it really. I think I stand out because of that. And that served me well as I've seen results from approaching things differently.

Chapter Ten

Cultivate Influential Industry Relationships

The most important part of any community development is the influence you bring to that community. When you're first getting started, influence needs to be borrowed before you can build it yourself.

There are always people who you look up to in your industry. **Find a way to build a relationship with those people who've already done the work that you are looking to do.**

The road to a personal brand is a long journey. Learning from other people who've already done the work ahead of you will help you speed your journey along as you can avoid their mistakes and gain an advantage from the tips that they've picked up along the way.

To interact with more influential industry thought leaders, identify those people. Organize your list of thought leaders based on your opportunity to meet those people. The biggest influencers will be the hardest to reach. Your current network will be the easiest to reach. And then there will be everyone in between.

If you can't start with the biggest influencers in your industry, reach out to less influential friends of those people. Find ways to get to know the network around your ideal influencers. Think of it like this: If you are an astronaut in space trying to get to the sun but can't reach it, then get as close to it as possible. Find a planet that's closer to the sun than you are and go there instead. The more influence someone has, the harder they will be to reach.

> When I say influencer, I don't mean someone who has built a large online following. I mean someone who's built a reputation for themselves as a leader in your industry. They may have a following online, but that's not the only criteria.

There are three reasons you should look to cultivate influential industry relationships, the first of which is that you can learn from the most knowledgeable people in your industry.

Learn from the Established Experts and Influencers in Your Industry

Wisdom comes from experience. Don't limit yourself to learning from your own experience. Learn from the experiences of others. The best thing to do to get started down this path is to **be insanely curious about the people around you**. As you start to listen to your curiosity, figure out where you can participate in the places where those influencers are engaging. Maybe they have an online community or content that you can engage with. See if they have a program that you can join, whether it's free or paid, or a course that you can take. Find an event where they are speaking that you can attend.

Get to know the work of influencers in your industry. Learn from the knowledge they distill. If they wrote a book, read the book. Understand what they are focusing on creating. Listen to the things that they are talking about. Pay attention to the opinions that they're developing.

The closer you can get to the experts and influencers in your industry, the more opportunities you'll have to see behind the scenes. Sometimes, we only get to see the finished product of other people's efforts. To see how they got there you must dig deeper, uncover the story, find the failures and learnings, and take in their journey, not just their destination.

One great way to do this is to **find ways to ask questions and get answers specific to where you are on your journey**. One of my favorite ways to do this is to either invite people on to your podcast for an interview or to join a paid mastermind with the people you want to learn from.

In a podcast interview, you get sixty minutes to ask every question you want to ask. And the person you're interviewing gets a little exposure to your audience. If you don't have a podcast, start one! You can also create your own YouTube channel in a matter of minutes these days and post your content there. Or at least start a blog, and tell your guest that the interview will live on your blog.

In a paid mastermind, you are paying to join someone's group with the promise of learning from them directly. There are typically live weekly or monthly calls where you get to ask questions, and you get to be a part of a group of people who are on the same journey as you.

Oftentimes, masterminds also give you access to online courses you can learn from as well as other resources, templates, or tools that you could use. To find a mastermind, start by making a list of thought leaders in your industry, and see if they have any courses or groups you can join. You can also search for Facebook groups on your topic as bigger groups are usually connected to a paid mastermind.

You don't have to reinvent the wheel. When you're building your personal brand, look at the models that have already been developed. Use a model that has already started to work, and apply it to your own unique experience.

Leverage Influential Relationships as Social Proof

The second reason you should cultivate influential industry relationships when you're building your personal brand is to leverage social proof. As those relationships develop, they can become social proof of your influence and expertise.

If you personally know the number one influencer in your industry, then people will associate some of their influence with you.

The more relationships you can build with influencers, the more likely you are to run in the circles that people look up to. Typically, most people prefer to be in the audience rather than in the limelight. If they go to an event, they like to watch the people on stage. If they go to a Facebook group, they like to watch people saying things in the comments. If they go to a social channel, they like to watch the content that's being created.

You can **differentiate yourself simply by being a creator and a participant rather than a watcher**. This will bring watchers into your world. Those relationships you develop with the influential people in your industry become social proof for your brand and give you clout.

Influencers are hard to reach. They don't just talk to and make friends with anybody. But if you put in the work to build the right relationships with those people, that work will pay for itself. Not everybody's going to like you or want to be in your circle of relationships, but the ones that do will bring their community, influence, and knowledge with them.

All of that could benefit you over time. All it takes is for you to enter those relationships with the mindset of being someone who gives to and invests in them and thinks about them as a long-term investment.

Those relationships will not develop overnight. These types of relationships are slow to develop with small doses of consistent, applied attention and intention.

Every time you can be around someone who is influential in your industry, use it to make another deposit into that relationship. As someone starts to see you interacting in their environment, community, and in their world, over a long period of time, they notice you. With the right commitment, it is unavoidable that you'll build some type of relationship with that person.

Whether that relationship is a friendship or just mutual respect and understanding, it is still a beneficial investment of your time.

Meet the Friends of Your Influential Friends

The third reason you should cultivate influential industry relationships is that those people are connected to more people that you can meet or serve. If they've been around longer than you, they have more relationships. As you get to know people like that, and as those relationships develop for you, oftentimes, you'll naturally end up meeting the friends of your influential friends.

These relationships can translate into more people seeing you because of that proximity. Just like any relationship, their followers become your followers. Their friends become your friends. And they all start to see you more often.

When more people notice you, they become curious about you. There are more chances for them to see what you are up to. If they can see you and what you're doing, they can see if you are a fit for them. They may even be looking for the help that you provide.

Anytime that you can go from having low exposure to high exposure in an area, it's going to help your personal brand. The best place to start is with the people who have already cultivated those communities.

Lean in to find influential industry relationships and see what happens. Get to know people who've already developed communities, and you might start to see that some of those people want to join your community as well.

Activity Break: Set Up Your Partnering Plan

Start setting up your partnering plan. Go to BrandonBirkmeyer.com/FCL.

Starting Your Dream 100 Partner List

- Look at the people you've already met and the relationships you already have, and write down the people who are leaders, experts, influencers, or connectors. We'll call this your "dream 100 partner list."

- Look at people in your industry, and make a list of the ones you'd like to know better, even if they seem impossible to connect with.

- Expand your list by looking at who these people are connected with on social media and who they follow. Add those people to your list too if you find them interesting.

- Organize your list into three groups (easy, medium, hard) based on how easy it would be to meet them. Fill in any gaps.

Engaging with Your Partner List

- Go online and follow the social media and content channels of people on your partner list. See what they are posting, and engage with their content in an authentic way.

- Take note of any common interests and any events that they may be attending or speaking at that you may be interested in attending.

Your Partnership Offers

- Offer a fifteen-to-thirty-minute "get to know you" chat.

- Offer to interview someone on your show or to feature them in content.

- Offer to share a relevant referral or resource.

- Offer to follow their content or social media channels.

- Offer some sort of help or service.

Your Outreach Plan

- Attend relevant events in your industry, where you can meet people from your partner list.

- Follow up at events and after events with attendees, introducing yourself.

- Ask your friends or contacts for relevant introductions.

- Invite people you've connected with to a "get to know you" call. If they are a bigger influencer or expert, invite them to an interview for your blog, podcast, or YouTube channel.

Interview with Travis Chappell

IG: @TRAVISCHAPPELL

Travis Chappell is a former door-to-door salesman turned founder, investor, speaker, and podcaster. He is the founder and CEO of Guestio .com, the highest quality guest and show booking marketplace in the industry. He's also the cohost of the top-ranked podcasts *Travis Makes Friends* and *Figuring It Out*.

In addition to interviewing people like Shaquille O'Neal, Rob Dyrdek, Dane Cook, Grant Cardone, Josh Peck, Molly Bloom, Jasmine Star, John Maxwell, Michael Hyatt, Kevin Harrington, Dean Graziosi, and hundreds of others, he has been a guest on top podcasts like *Bigger Pockets*, *EOFire*, and *Born to Impact*. Travis has been featured in *Forbes, Entrepreneur, TechCrunch, Bloomberg*, and dozens of other media outlets.

Have Cool Conversations with Cool People

Brandon Birkmeyer: When you started this, what made you want to create a podcast about networking and relationships?

Travis Chappell: Yeah, good question. I figured out first that I wanted to do a podcast, and then I didn't know what I was going to podcast about. I had a background in door-to-door sales, and that was my only expertise.

When I was done with door-to-door sales, looking for my next move, I was considering everything and listening to podcasts, and I just kind of thought about the idea of starting one. It seemed interesting to have cool conversations with people who are out doing amazing things and crushing it in life or in business, whatever it was. So, when I decided to start the show, I was like, *well, what am I going to talk about?*

The topic of networking made sense to me. If I want to get to the seven-figure mark, I should probably go hang out with seven-figure entrepreneurs. And so, the networking thing fell in my lap.

I wanted to learn how to do it better myself because I wanted to get good guests on my show. Then I was like, *how am I going to get good guests on my show?* Probably through some sort of networking; probably through some sort of relationship building, connecting, or getting warm introductions to other people.

My whole thought process was if I could get into somebody's inner circle, then I wouldn't ever have to pay to get somebody to be on my show. It's not going to cost money if you talk to the right person because everybody will do stuff for close enough friends and family.

So, if I can figure out a way to build relationships and connections with all these other people, then it's just going to start building on itself. I didn't have proof, but it made sense in my mind and was something that I went forward and attacked head-on.

Use Your Platform to Add Value to Your Relationships

Brandon Birkmeyer: What are some of the core tenets of relationship building and networking?

Travis Chappell: Yeah, first and most importantly, you have to be a giver. You must learn how to give without the expectation of receiving anything in return.

Always try to be giving at least fifty-one percent of the value in every relationship that you have. And I know that doesn't sound like a secret, but seriously, that's really what it is. All I've done is given a ton to people and not expected anything back. The universe will always reward that. Even if that person won't reward it directly, it doesn't matter. I'm not doing it for that.

The universe will always bring it back. It's just a simple law of attraction. The first thing that I always tell people is to give, and to give without the expectation of receiving anything in return. That's number one and most important on the list.

As far as going forward, your positioning is super important. One of the most important ways to position yourself is to build your own platform. If you truly want to explode your network, start a podcast tomorrow. I promise you, if you start a podcast and you start interviewing people, your network will take off and grow exponentially. The number one thing that I did to build the network that I have now is start my podcast.

Having a show, like this one now, that has decent traction, a good guest list, and a good reputation, is a value-add piece that allows me to connect with people I want to connect with.

I think you need to have some mental shifts before you jump into this journey.

1. Be a giver.

2. Think long term, not transactionally.

3. Stop thinking of people as contacts, and start thinking of people as people.

These are a few mindset shifts that have to be done right off the bat that will help you get through this process a lot easier.

Build Relationships with Influential People

Brandon Birkmeyer: How do you choose which people to invest your time with?

Travis Chappell: I'm glad you brought that up because you need to pick people who you would like to add more value to, such as people that are in a specific industry or who have influence. Make sure that they're top people in your field and that they're connected to a ton of other people in your industry.

I think that was one of the best decisions that I made. I made it accidentally. It was not something that was super thought out. I just liked John Lee Dumas a lot and was like, *I want to connect with the guy because he's a super successful podcaster, and if I rub shoulders with him, I'll learn how to do it properly.*

That was true, but also, he's a super well-connected dude. He has thousands of episodes on his show, and all of them are interviews. A lot of people know who this guy is. I invested heavily into a relationship with John that benefited my knowledge base and my network. An introduction from John Lee Dumas to somebody else is much, much more powerful than me just reaching out and being like, "Hey, what's up?"

Chapter Eleven

Find and Win High Profile Engagement Opportunities

O nce you become more active in the communities around you, you'll see and feel the benefits of participation. You can increase your knowledge, build new friendships, or find ways to practice and improve your skills in your industry.

For those people who want to build personal brands, **one of the fastest ways to develop a community is to step into leadership roles** in any organization. Anytime you are participating in a community, the work you can do to move from participant to someone who's highly engaged will set you apart in terms of the attention you get. That attention will lead to community for you and attention for your ideas.

Establish an Active Leadership Presence

Start by establishing an active leadership presence. Every community you participate in has opportunities to lead. Note that leadership can take many forms. Sometimes, it's an opportunity to lead a conversation, ask a question, or offer advice. Other times, an active leadership presence means volunteering to play a role in the communities or organizations that you're participating in.

Every community needs people to keep that community running. Each year, there are positions that open up that you can volunteer for. Many organizations actively ask and never have enough people volunteering to participate. That leaves an opportunity for you to be the person who takes on that active leadership role.

These leadership roles tend to be high-visibility positions. The people that are in the community get to see you more often. The new people that enter the community as first-time members or new participants come into it seeing you as a leader in the community. These roles position you as someone worth paying attention to.

The best way to be a leader in an organization is to **start by engaging the current leadership to ask how you can help them** with the commitments that leadership entails.

> Now, I'm not saying this is easy. It's a time commitment and takes work. The work you put in helping and serving the leadership of an organization will always come back to you either as goodwill from the leaders themselves or as an invitation for you to participate as a leader yourself.

Leaders take initiative. Everyone recognizes that initiative is what people need to move the agenda of an organization forward. Be someone who takes initiative and participates.

Engage with People of Influence

Every time you reach out to people who already have communities, it's an opportunity for you to position yourself as someone who can serve that community. And, sometimes, it requires you to ask to serve.

No one will know you have a set of ideas and expertise that you like to speak about and teach unless you tell them. Engage with people of influence, and offer to teach those things to their communities Many professional speakers started to build their speaking careers by actively pitching themselves repeatedly.

There are opportunities within nationally networked organizations. Every industry has associations that try to move the industry forward. Those associations have a national presence and are locally managed. That means, if you can find a way to engage with people of influence at your local association, that might lead to opportunities for you to engage with people in other chapters and other organizations throughout the country.

You can start by getting involved in your home city and offering to help and connect with people of influence there. That can lead you to introductions or recommendations to engage with people in other places.

The more you can engage with people of influence, the better chance you'll have to find and win high-profile engagement opportunities. The people of influence already have all the relationships you need with the people who run all the other events and organizations. Lean in and make the ask, and let them know what you like to help people with.

Take the Stage Everywhere, All the Time

Once you've started to let people know how you help, you also want to make sure you let them know that you have a certain idea that you like to present and that presentation can come through in lots of forms and formats.

Sometimes, it's a workshop you like to run that helps people engage in your idea. Other times, it's a presentation that would help. It can be a freebie, a resource, or a webinar. You can find keynote speaking opportunities or a chance to MC or move an event along as a host. **Any chance you can find to take the stage is going to help you build your personal brand.**

On stage, you are standing in front of an audience who's giving you their attention. Make sure you record yourself giving these presentations. The easiest, fastest way to get more opportunities to take the stage is to have examples of you taking the stage.

Usually that comes in the form of video footage of you on the stage, giving your presentations. In the beginning, you'll need to be creative in finding ways to have people help you record and edit those videos into something worth watching.

All you need is a minute or less of a great quality clip you can add to a few other clips to create a demo reel. That demo reel shows your ability to take the stage and deliver a message to an audience.

When you're starting out, a lot of those opportunities will be free, unpaid speaking engagements. But those free, unpaid speaking engagements may have audience members who can refer you or book you to speak for a future paid opportunity.

Even if that's not the case, at least the audience is listening to you, giving you their attention, and they can be recruited to become part of your community in some way.

When you have this stage, not only can you teach and share your ideas, but you also get to introduce yourself to people. **Let them know who you are and how they can connect with you.** Leverage the power of storytelling to clearly articulate how you can serve them beyond that one speaking opportunity.

This is networking at the fastest pace. Instead of speaking to people one-on-one, you are now speaking to many people at the same time. The follow-up will be you showing interest in them and seeing if you can build the relationship beyond the stage. It all starts with you finding those high-profile engagement opportunities and winning the chance to speak. Then leverage the power of storytelling to deliver a clear idea of who you are and how you help.

Activity Break: Set Up Your Speaking Profile

Get started setting up your speaking profile. This profile can live on your website, blog page, or on a listing site for public speakers. Here are a few places to start. These worksheets are available at BrandonBirkmeyer.com/FCL.

Your Headline

- In a short sentence, describe who you are and how you help. This can be your job title (i.e., marketing strategist for startups) or your vision of success (i.e., "Speed up your sales cycle and win bigger contracts").

Your Biography

- Write one paragraph that clearly describes your expertise and experience. Describe some of the work you've been doing lately. Keep it current and relevant to who would book you to speak.

- Include some bullet points about what the audience's key takeaways will be when they hear you speak.

Your Speaking Topics

- Brainstorm an initial list of topics relevant to your experience and the audience you are speaking to. Reduce the list to your favorite three to five topics.

- Write out a simple title for your speech such as "How to..." or "The 5 Steps to...". Then personalize the title with wordplay or some descriptive words that stand out and align with your personality.

Your Showcase

- Share some pictures and/or videos of you on the stage. Include links to any presentations you'd like to share, if relevant.

- Share links to any podcasts, articles, or books you've participated in.

Your Credibility

- Highlight your history and ability with any testimonials you've received and other PR that features you.

Interview with Tamsen Webster

IG: @TAMSENWEBSTER

T ED Talks are stages that have become popular in person and through viral online videos. They are influential speeches with great storytelling from expert speakers on education, business, science, tech, and creativity. Tamsen Webster is a former TEDx executive producer and current idea strategist. If you've ever seen a TEDx presentation that's gone viral, you could look to someone like her to figure out how they did it.

Tamsen was named a thinker to watch in the Thinkers50 Radar Class of 2022. She's the author of *Find Your Red Thread: Make Your Big Ideas Irresistible*. She describes herself as part strategist, part storyteller, part English-to-English translator, and she helps experts drive action with their ideas.

Speak on as Many Stages as Possible

Brandon Birkmeyer: How did you get into the professional speaking industry?

Tamsen Webster: I'm a big fan of what my husband and I call free noting, which is speaking for free to generate business but not selling from the stage. In the middle of that, and in the middle of agency life, I had a friend of mine, who happened to be the executive director of TEDx Cambridge, ask me if I wanted to be the executive producer.

He asked, "Can you take what you do as a speaker yourself and help other people figure out how to do that?" I was not a speaker coach, but I knew some stuff that I'd learned, and I could share from that. That's where I started a deep dive into storytelling.

Practice the Art of Storytelling

Brandon Birkmeyer: What would you say is the reason that storytelling is so difficult, and what keeps people from using it in their business more?

Tamsen Webster: I think that we focus more on the form of story than the function of those elements. Two things can happen if you think story equals "the hero's journey" exclusively, which it doesn't. The hero's journey is one structure of a very common story. That's why it's a good first place to go. But it can also be limiting.

First off, a true hero's journey is seven to twelve steps. And for your average business storyteller, whether that's a leader, entrepreneur, or marketing person, figuring out how your thing fits into all seven to twelve steps is a lot.

Also, a hero's journey is about a very specific thing. It's about a person who wants a thing that must overcome the odds to get that thing. Then, the hero is the one who saves the day. This implies a lot. It implies that the hero can actually solve this thing, that they are the only one who can save the day, and that there is one solution that can solve the problem.

I do a lot of work with experts, people who are founding impact-based startups and nonprofits and folks like that. One of the things that makes it so difficult is that there isn't a villain and we're not the hero. For example, one person can't solve climate change. So, how can we possibly make this work?

What ends up happening is people throw their arms up and think it doesn't work. They go back to bullet points and data. That's super frustrating to me because story can be such a powerful way to get your message across cleanly, clearly, without distortion, and with maximum understanding.

Who doesn't want that? But when you're trying to use a form that doesn't fit your situation, it can feel like there's nothing out there for you. That was a main reason why I wanted to take the approach that I did when I started to tackle this idea of storytelling.

My approach was to look at the elements present in every kind of story. There are only five—only four of which are super critical. It became a way that we could take complicated information and make it feel like a story.

We could tell stories that didn't have endings. We could tell stories that weren't reliant on a single hero or a single solution. We could tell stories that were appropriate to the scale of problems, both big and small.

I wanted to figure out how to turn this into something, where it didn't feel like a very heavy lift but could also be framed in the form of questions that people could answer. For example, what question is your audience asking that your product or service answers? What's the real reason that they're not getting that answer from currently available options? What do you believe about that problem that makes your solution the only one that makes sense to you?

Then we can align with something that your audience already agrees with. And finally, it all adds up to the big change in thinking or behavior that your idea represents. Those are the four things.

1. What do people want?

2. Why aren't they getting it now?

3. How am I looking at this differently?

4. Why do I think that's the right way to look at it?

And those questions, although they may not always be easy to answer, are straightforward. They are in line with the way that business owners, marketers, salespeople, and entrepreneurs already think.

That's how people are thinking because you need those pieces of information to make anything make sense. It's an excavation process of going back, rediscovering what your own thought process was behind your product or service, and reconstructing it so that someone else can follow a similar line of thinking to get to your same position.

It even works for folks that don't consider themselves to be natural story-tellers. We are all storytellers, by the way, but we must put it into a format that people feel comfortable with so they can get the maximum benefit.

Listen to the full interviews at BrandonBirkmeyer.com/FCL.

Making an Impact

The last piece of the personal branding puzzle is making an impact. This is where you determine what your offer should be—something tangible and transformative. Solve a problem that creates a change in someone's everyday life.

Your offer can come in a variety of formats. Done-for-you services are easy to sell when you are starting a business. Or you can implement coaching and training programs for individuals or small groups. Consider building digital products such as digital courses, guides, and templates. You can also make an impact with your content and ideas.

If you are working within an organization, think of your offers as the projects that you take on that build your resume and reputation. As you make offers to solve problems within the organization, your success builds credibility. The impact of your solutions is felt by everyone you work with and your star will rise.

As your credibility grows, you get to decide how you leverage it. You can put your name in the hat for that next promotion. The doors may be open for you to pursue new jobs or outside opportunities. You may be interested in a side hustle, freelancing, or working for yourself. All of this is possible as you prove your value to other people.

Many personal brand businesses start with creating content, but some never get past that initial step. They jump straight into a personal brand business such as coaching, consulting, speaking, training, creating courses, or freelancing. I challenge you to keep it small, simple, and easy to understand, especially if you're just starting. Pick something easy that you can help people with right now.

For example, if you are a marketing consultant, pick one or two things to focus on within marketing, such as email marketing and content writing. Pick something easy, singular, and tangible that isn't just coaching or strategy.

Offer a simple done-for-you service that people need help with right now. The reason you want to start with something like that is to start creating impact quickly. This allows you to find people you can serve based on your existing skill set and knowledge base, so you can start helping people right away.

This puts you in a business building and service mindset. It takes all your energy and faces it outward. That energy can be used to solve problems for clients. Along the way, you can decide what direction to head in as you gain momentum.

You may have many great ideas, but **you can waste hours, days, or even months trying to build a business in your head**. Avoid the common startup problem of analysis paralysis. Avoid internalizing your business. Don't sit at home creating logos and mocking up websites and cool offers. Get out there and start networking, meeting people, and having conversations. Based on those conversations, you'll find opportunities to make offers. Make offers to help based on things you can do that are small and tangible.

Relationships start with a series of small steps that build trust. As you serve people over time, you'll build more credibility and reputation in your industry. The more people you help, the more you can evolve and grow how you're helping them. Then you can start to bake in bigger and better ways to serve with your business.

As the demand increases for your services and your time starts to get crunched, your offers will change. When the demand for your time is more than the hours you have available in your day, you can raise your rates or bring in team members. You can elevate your services or automate and digitize your products.

Let demand dictate the offer, but **first make an impact, even if that means that you're helping people for free**. It's okay to start with free offers. Use those free offers in the beginning to build your reputation. Find people you can barter with and trade with—*I'll help you with this service, and maybe you can build my website.*

Sometimes, they can even refer you to clients. Every person you meet has the potential to introduce you to five or six more customers. Put your energy into creating goodwill and finding clients who would love to refer you to their friends. Make an impact and watch your reputation grow.

There are three steps to making an impact with your personal brand:

- Start with quick, deliberate wins

- Grab attention with distinct, visionary campaigns

- Lead your industry with progressive movements

Follow these steps to build credibility with your audience through deliberate, value-creating actions that make an impact.

Chapter Twelve

Start with Quick, Deliberate Wins

When you're just getting started building your personal brand, one of the goals with your audience is to make an impact in their life or business. The impact is the most important part, but transformation takes time.

When you first meet somebody or when someone first comes across your ideas or your content, they may not have the time to spend going through your full transformation process. You may not even have a "full transformation process" built yet! This is why it's important to start with things that are quick and deliberate in terms of delivering a win for that person.

Quick Wins Save Time

Another reason I like to start with a quick, deliberate win is that **people don't have time to waste and are looking for simple solutions**.

Now, you may find this funny, but in one of my first jobs, working at an ice cream shop, we used to make a lot of banana splits. I learned how to cut a banana with a knife very quickly to take the peel off and slice the banana into small circles to put into an ice cream dessert. It's not the hardest thing to learn, and it's a pretty fun trick.

When I talk to my son, who's seven years old, about opening a banana, he's not looking for something that's complicated. In fact, it's obvious how to open a banana. But, every now and then, he gets a banana that's a little tough to open and needs help.

I could teach my son the more complicated way to open a banana with a knife. It's interesting, and maybe he'll use it in a fancy dessert in the future, but right now, he's hungry! He just needs a quick win.

When you're just getting started, sometimes the simple solution is the best solution. Anytime you are building relationships with an audience, starting simple is the easiest way to get their attention. Provide a solution to one of their many problems in a fast and easy way.

> There are lots of ideas that you've come across, resources that you've used, or knowledge that you've acquired that someone may need and that can be shared in an easy-to-digest way. Start to accumulate your ideas, resources, and solutions. Turn them into easy products that you can give to people you come across.

Now, it's easier than ever to share your knowledge digitally. You can create easy-to-download worksheets, checklists, forms, and even easy-to-access videos and tutorials. If designed correctly, it shouldn't take more than a couple of minutes for someone to access and act on your solution.

If your solution helps someone do something faster, smarter, or better than before, you can win a little confidence with that person. But you must start with something simple. People don't have time to try big, transformational ideas with someone that they've never met before.

Quick Wins Build Trust

Another important reason why you should start with a quick, deliberate win—trust. Quick wins build trust and credibility more quickly.

For example, if you are a new manager entering a corporation, you are building trust from scratch. Let's say you wanted to implement a large organizational change. It could take six months to implement and train and get working. The results of that change may take an additional six to twelve months to see. What that means is that in those first six months you're getting work done, but no one is seeing it.

That means that, in the first six months, there are no wins. And what if, in those six months, it doesn't work? That's a lot of time to waste on something, and you've missed the opportunity to build any goodwill along the way.

However, if within the first three days of showing up to a new job you implemented some very simple, quick wins, it shows success and builds trust. If your ideas save the team a little bit of time, help make their jobs a little bit easier, improve communication on the team, or just generally make their work better, it's a win that gets noticed. **Even small, incremental progress gets noticed and builds trust.** Your wins establish your credibility and prove that you know how to create solutions for your team and business.

After you lock in some small wins, you can share slightly larger plans and ideas. For example, if your second idea is going to take one week or one month to implement, the team will trust you to succeed again. You have already proven yourself to be useful. Then, if you deliver something useful again, you can take even more risk and implement bigger plans.

Trust will keep growing because you've already proven that you could do it in shorter amounts of time. Find ways to get wins in your life, your content, and your business that start to build trust more quickly.

If you're building a coaching or consulting business and you want to create impact, find ways to help your clients solve one simple problem before you start pitching them on larger fixes. A great way to start is to host workshops where you teach one topic to a small group of clients. Help them make progress, show them a roadmap, and work with them in person. After the workshop, people who found it valuable will be more open to working with you in the future.

The more you serve and build trust, the more people will talk about you and your work. Don't underestimate the power of word-of-mouth, testimonials, and referrals. People get excited to share things that have helped them. The more you can do quickly to help people, the faster you will grow. **Credibility leads to referability.**

Quick Wins Show Your Value

Starting with quick, deliberate wins builds impact for your personal brand that actively demonstrates your value.

In a world where people often share similar titles, skills, experiences, and work histories, demonstrating your value can be very difficult. A quick, thoughtful, and deliberate win that speaks to the person that you're trying to help can go a long way in separating you from the competition.

The key word here is deliberate. To come up with a deliberate win, you do have to **do the work to understand the person you're trying to solve problems for.** Just because you've come up with a quick solution, doesn't make it the right solution for everybody. You can customize and personalize your wins to the individuals that are in front of you. What's great about small wins and quick wins is that they can be designed, and they don't take a lot of time to put together.

Come up with a few different ideas that might help a small group of people and demonstrate your value to them. Once you've demonstrated value, you start to be seen as a person of value in your industry.

Personal branding is a game of cumulative advances. The more deposits you can make into the goodwill box, the further you will go. The work you do, that shows your expertise and offers helpful solutions, makes deposits that add up to more impact in the future.

This is one of the best strategies to use when you are just getting started in your personal branding journey. There will be moments where you come up with larger solutions to larger problems, but that happens after the quick wins. You'll find full processes to take people from one end of the spectrum to another in terms of a transformation, but the quick wins come first.

Activity Break: Set Up Your Helpful Resources

Get started setting up your helpful resources. Here are a few places to start. These worksheets are available at BrandonBirkmeyer.com/FCL.

Resource Types

- Decide what type of resources will create simple wins for the people you want to support. Here are some examples:

  - Referrals – Share direct recommendations or lists you've created such as preferred partners, favorite websites/apps, book recommendations, industry updates, or research/resources.

  - Templates – Prebuild examples of processes and resources that you use on a regular basis like mock-ups, spreadsheets, calendars, scripts, presentations, or graphics.

  - Guides – List out your own instructions such as "how to" guides, checklists, step-by-step instructions, white papers, articles, quarterly reports, video tutorials, or digital courses.

  - Tools – Provide tool recommendations or build your own tools such as assessments, calculators, quizzes, spreadsheets, or automation.

Formatting

- Use a graphic design tool like Canva to find premade designs to make your resources look better and more professional.

- Add your logo, contact information, and any copyright to your resources.

Accessibility

- Make the resources easy to share and download. Turn your resources into PDF documents, or upload them online for download from your webpage or a file-sharing site like Dropbox.

Promotion

- Talk about your resources on your website and on your social media profiles, and include links for access.

- Mention your resources in your email signature or in social media posts. Regularly remind people that you have ways to help them.

- When you meet people, follow up with your useful resources when relevant. Directly sending your resources to someone that needs it is the easiest way to be helpful.

Interview with Austin Armstrong

IG: @SOCIALTYPRO

Austin Armstrong is a lifelong digital marketer, public speaker, podcaster, and founder of Socialty Pro, an organic SEO and vertical video marketing agency, as well as a great example of someone who builds off of quick wins. He's also the CEO of Syllabi, which is a marketing tool that helps business owners create a social media content strategy in minutes.

Austin has posted over two and a half thousand videos on TikTok, tripling his business's revenue, and helped thousands more across his client's accounts. He's leveraged his success on TikTok to gain millions of followers across every social media platform, including seven hundred and fifty thousand followers on TikTok, seven hundred and sixty-four thousand followers on Instagram, and five hundred and seventy-nine thousand subscribers and over six million likes on YouTube.

Austin's business and brand started to take off when he found traction on TikTok with a series of videos describing *Insanely Useful Websites That Feel Illegal to Know*.

Leverage Quick Win Ideas That Already Exist

Brandon Birkmeyer: Where did you come up with the idea to share short videos about useful websites on your TikTok content?

Austin Armstrong: I've been sharing useful websites since I got started on TikTok and for the last four years. I mixed that in with SEO tips, which was the first thing that popped for me on TikTok. About two years ago, I was trying to innovate through different original but relatable styles on TikTok. The magic happens when you can level up something familiar and create something fresh to make it your own.

I didn't invent sharing useful websites. I've been doing it for a while, but people have been sharing website lists since the beginning of the internet. I also didn't invent the conversation style of talking to yourself on TikTok. But I was probably the first person to merge those two things and have that conversational style while showing useful websites.

It was something applicable to me, and it exploded. Quick side note here. It didn't explode immediately. It took a little time. I think I knocked out three videos in that style, and they did okay. One did around a hundred thousand views on TikTok, which is pretty good. The other ones flopped.

I disregarded the format for a couple of weeks or a month. Then I reposted the first video, and now it has over eleven million views on TikTok and about twenty million views on YouTube. I've been doubling down on that ever since—doing that style for about a year now. It works every time.

Brandon Birkmeyer: When did you go all in on short-form video? Was there a moment that hit you when it was clearly what you needed to do?

Austin Armstrong: When I started in October of 2019, I was one month in and not gaining traction. I was putting out cat videos and trying trends, with the occasional digital marketing tip. None of it worked because there was no cohesiveness to my channel—no reason to follow me. It was all over the place.

I attended a webinar from Rachel Pedersen, a great entrepreneur and TikTok creator. Something in her webinar really shifted my mind—how she framed things, almost as a search engine. She was very ahead of her time with that methodology.

Being in SEO, I could understand it. Just create content around what people are searching for. So, I gave myself an ultimatum: I would only create content around my business for thirty days straight. And if there was no traction, maybe it was not the platform or format for me.

A funny thing happens when you go all in and commit to something, giving yourself a deadline. You start to see traction. A week or two into that, a video had popped. It did a million views, which set the trajectory.

Then I did video responses to every single comment that came in on that video. I built a lot of traction and started to gain a large following with an engaged audience and leads. It was generating leads for my business. That's when I went all in, and I've never slowed down since. I'm close to three thousand videos posted on TikTok over the last four years.

Make Your Quick Wins Easy to Access

Brandon Birkmeyer: How do you pull people from being viewers of your social media into your actual business and world?

Austin Armstrong: Firstly, we must recognize that viewers are not stupid. They know how to look at your profile, and if they're interested, they know how to click on the link in your bio.

It starts at that point. In your bio, be descriptive. You have three lines. Share what you do, who you help, and where they can contact you. Just a simple format for your bio—as simple as possible. Reduce the steps and all the friction to make it easy to contact you.

I pivoted my approach to lead generation maybe six or seven months ago. The lead generator I thought people wanted, and that would grow my email list, was an SEO for business checklist. It was doing okay. It was collecting thirty to fifty emails a week, with spikes here and there if I promoted my email sign-up.

Then I started paying attention to what people were asking for in the comments. They were asking for a list of all the websites. In every video, I share three to five websites. It's a lot, so people were asking for a list. At some point, I made this list of websites available and asked for an email. As soon as I did that, it exploded. Now, I'm collecting around one to two thousand emails a week—a drastic increase.

People can get my list of most useful websites, which is my free lead magnet. But then there are also opportunities where they can book a one-on-one call with me for hourly consultations. Also, they can schedule a call with my team to hire my agency. They can buy digital products and digital downloads and courses that I have available.

As soon as they enter their email and subscribe, they're entered into an email campaign sequence that upsells some stuff and generates leads for us. I make it known that it's there and easy to find, then every now and then I sneak in a call to action.

Most of the time, I don't even mention it. I just have it in the description of the videos on those three platforms.

Chapter Thirteen

Grab Attention with Distinct, Visionary Campaigns

A campaign is an organized course of action to achieve a goal. When looking to build impact for your personal brand, oftentimes, you must think on a project-by-project basis. A campaign is a great way to build a particular project or solve a particular problem.

The benefit of campaigns is that they tend to contain themselves in a particular part of a process. For example, if you were teaching people how to bake a cake and you wanted to separate that into steps, the first part may be getting all your ingredients together. The second part might be mixing the materials. And the third could be the actual baking of the cake.

If you wanted to isolate one step, you could pick one to focus on and dive deeper into it. For baking a cake, you could just choose the first part—only discussing the assembling of the ingredients. Focusing gives you more options. You could explore ingredients that are lower cost or items that are around the house. You could review ingredients that are seasonal or from a certain part of the world. You could talk about organic ingredients or more healthy ingredients. The list goes as far as your imagination.

Campaigns Provide a Meaningful Solution

Campaigns reduce your scope of work to just one goal which helps you focus on finding a singular, meaningful solution. That solution demonstrates that you understand and can help with a very specific problem your audience is facing.

It helps you to be clearer to your audience in terms of your area of expertise and focus. If you offer to help people with many different things, it can be confusing for them. Your audience doesn't know where to start with you. **Providing a more focused, meaningful solution helps define your identity within your industry.**

You can choose the part of the process that leans most into your strengths or your passions. Whatever your interests are within a particular process, you can lean into that. You can become someone who has done more research, has more experience, or shares more ideas about that one part of the process.

Niching down in this way can allow you to explore lots of different ideas in a smaller space. It's hard to know everything about everything. It is easier to become an expert in something when you contain your focus to a particular set of steps or parts of a process. This is true for any industry.

This doesn't have to be your full year focus—short campaigns are useful. You might have one project you dive into at the beginning of the year, and then in the second half of the year, you focus on a different project entirely. That gives you opportunities to constantly be promoting and talking about one thing at a time.

For example, during the month of February, you could talk about a project that you are executing in March. Every time someone hears from you, that's what they're thinking about. They're not thinking of everything you can do. They're focused on that one project that you could help them with.

Then, maybe in July, you start talking about a different idea, and you promote it for the whole month. In August, you execute that idea for that month. Now, your audience has a second, very clear idea of how you help people.

Providing a meaningful solution that is project-based allows you to focus your messaging, audience, and solution in a very effective way. This gives people an opportunity to figure out how they could be helped by you during one, specific part of a process. A successful outcome can lead to someone wanting to work with you again and again on lots of different parts of the process and potentially becoming a full-time partner, client, or service provider.

Campaigns Are Clear and Obvious

The second way to grab attention with distinct, visionary campaigns is to make it clear and obvious how you go through and implement your solution.

People want to understand your idea as soon as you begin explaining it. They also want to know how you will teach the idea and then how the implementation of that idea will happen. **It's your job to articulate the idea, the mode, and the method of your solution.**

Anytime you're teaching something, the clearer and more obvious you can make it, the easier it is for the audience to say yes. A clear idea demonstrates a solution to a simple problem for your audience. It shows them a before and an after; then they get to decide if that's the type of solution that they are looking for. They are deciding if your idea sounds like something that could work for them. This only works if it's specific and speaks to their exact problem.

The mode of your solution lets the audience know how they will be receiving your information. Will you be sharing it in a video? Is it something they'll have to read? Is it a workshop where there's some interaction? Will it be reading and then a coaching call? The mode of delivery will work for some people and not others.

There are different types of customers out there. And some of them may want a service or solution that you don't provide. You get to decide what you offer.

Some people design digital courses and offer coaching and implementation programs. The audience can choose what works best for them. Some people prefer self-study courses and just want to know the information. Other people want a training solution where they have the information but also get to ask questions along the way.

There's a third group of people who want you to do all the work for them. They want a fully-buttoned-up solution, and they simply want to outsource the work to you. Figuring out the mode that works best for your audience, or designing your product in a way that serves all of them and prices itself accordingly, is how you deliver a distinct, visionary campaign.

Your audience wants to hear what the steps of your solution are. These steps should also be clear and obvious. You can break most solutions into five or six steps. This may not contain every small step along the process, but five or six big steps will help them understand what happens first, middle, and last when they are trying to work through a solution with you.

Having a method that explains your step-by-step process lets your audience know that you have a plan. And if that plan makes sense to them, it gives them more confidence to say yes and to come on the journey with you.

Having a method also lets your audience know if this solution is going to cover everything they need. If you have five steps but they're missing two steps that are the most important for this audience, they may need to go somewhere else for a solution. If you never explain your steps, or your method, then the audience won't have enough information to say yes or no to your solution.

Campaigns Are Timely

Not every solution is right at every time of year, so you must make your campaigns timely. Some projects will be evergreen, but a lot of projects that you come up with will be seasonal. Some will work better at certain times of the year compared to others.

For example, goal-setting projects tend to happen at the beginning of someone's year, whereas implementation projects tend to happen in the middle. And evaluation and audit processes tend to happen at the end of a year.

You get to **speak to the timeliness of your solution and align it with the time of year that it tends to be needed** the most. And this will vary by industry and by project. Figure out if you're going to talk about a project for a set period of time, such as a month. Determine which month makes the most sense for this project. Align your solution with the time of year that people tend to be looking for that solution.

For example, if you're selling Christmas decorations for December, June seems like the wrong time to be promoting it because people aren't thinking about Christmas decorations in June (most of them, anyway).

There are projects that make sense year-round, and that's okay too. In those cases, you can still pick a time of year to focus your energy on running your campaign. Place your attention on that one thing, and give it everything you can to get the word out to your followers. It's hard to push at one hundred percent every day of the year.

You can still make an evergreen project timely. Look at your schedule and allocate your effort where it makes sense. For example, if a strategic project runs in February, you might need the month of March to focus on implementation. Then, if April is usually busy with other one-off projects and events, you can set that month aside as well. Then, the next campaign or solution would be available to push out in June or July.

And then August comes around, but you need another month off because school is starting back up for your kids and you're busy. So, the next time you're available to put a campaign out isn't until October. Check your schedule, and start to lay out your calendar with these campaigns.

The timeliness of an evergreen project is flexible to either when your audience needs a solution and is looking for it or to when you are best available to put it out there and implement it. Either way, it's better to focus your energy on a project to a particular timeframe to get the most out of it.

Your energy is not infinite. Focusing that energy makes it stronger. For example, if you were releasing a new book that you had just written, you may find ten partners to help promote your book. If those ten partners all promoted you in the same week, that's a lot of attention all at once. This is a good thing for a launch.

If you spread those ten promotions across the year, that attention is also spread out which creates less immediate impact and buzz for your book. It's better to focus those promotions on one or two specific periods of time. This reduces your workload to a contained time of year, removes distractions, and allows for more focused energy.

Activity Break: Set Up Your Solution Framework

Get started setting up your solution framework. Here are a few places to start. These worksheets are available at BrandonBirkmeyer.com/FCL.

Solution Brainstorm

- Find problems to solve. Keep a journal or list of problems you find and solutions you think of on a daily or weekly basis.

- Put time on your calendar to review that list at least once every three months.

- Pick a problem, and write it down on a post-it note. Then, add potential solution ideas on post-it notes and place them up next to your problem.

Method of Delivery

- When you're done adding your ideas, organize them into a step-by-step process.

Mode of Operation

- Decide what format best delivers your solution. For example, is it a downloadable file, or is it a series of videos, or maybe both. Maybe it's an in-person training or event. Determine what you need to make, how you want to present it, and over what timeframe.

Presenting the Offer

- In the beginning, share your solution with a small group of people. See if it helps them, and get their feedback on what they like and how to make it better.

- When sharing the offer more broadly, tell people about the value and benefits your solution provides and share testimonials of how it worked for others.

- Block off time on your calendar to promote the solution across your channels. Hold off on sharing the features, details, and pricing. First, ask people if they'd like more information about your offer and how your solution works. Then follow up.

Interview with Grant Baldwin

IG: @GBALDWIN

G rant Baldwin is a nationally-known speaker, podcaster, and author who has helped thousands of people start and build their speaking businesses through his Booked & Paid to Speak training course. He's also a great example of someone who uses distinct, visionary campaigns. Despite starting his speaking career with no audience, no following, and no network, he earned over two million dollars from over five hundred paid engagements all over the world. He's done everything from closed-door workshops to keynotes in front of more than thirteen thousand people. He did all of that without using traditional booking agents or speaker bureaus.

In 2015, he founded The Speaker Lab to give people the resource that he wished he had when he began his speaker journey (www.thespeakerlab.com). He's also the author of the book *The Successful Speaker*, and he has a podcast called *The Speaker Lab* which has published over three hundred episodes and has been downloaded over one and a half million times. He is regularly featured in the national media, including *Forbes*, *Inc.*, *Entrepreneur*, and *HuffPost*.

One Focus at a Time

Brandon Birkmeyer: How did you get started in building your personal brand?

Grant Baldwin: I started off as a full-time speaker. I was doing sixty to seventy paid gigs a year. I was speaking all over the U.S. and absolutely loved it.

I had a friend tell me early on that speaking is a high-paying manual labor job. You get paid really, really well to stand up on stage and run your mouth.

It's a cool job, a fun job, but at the same time, it is a job. I was wired toward having a business and entrepreneurship, and something that didn't entirely depend on me. So, as a speaker, I started looking around and figuring out if I wanted to do something else.

A lot of people were regularly asking me how to become a speaker. When I got started, I had those same questions. Because speaking, for so many people, is this mysterious black box. That's when we started doing some coaching and training around that. Initially, it was some stuff that was under my own personal brand.

Over time, as it continued to build and grow and evolve, we created a separate entity: The Speaker Lab. We started doing that, and as it took off, we continued to hire people and grow that side of it. That's when we became the core of who we are.

Brandon Birkmeyer: How did you decide where and when to focus your message and efforts?

Grant Baldwin: One of the more important parts and one of the most challenging parts of being a speaker, especially early on, is getting clarity on who you speak to and what problem you solve for that audience.

The mistake a lot of speakers make is to try and spread the net as far and wide as possible. This is not exclusive to just speakers. This is any type of personal brand. Sometimes, I'll ask speakers, "What do you speak about?" And they say, "Well, what do you want me to speak about?"

That doesn't work. You want to be the steakhouse and not the buffet. Meaning, if you and I are going out to eat, and we're looking for a good steak, we have a choice. We could go to a buffet, where steak is one of a hundred things that they offer, and they're all mediocre. Or we could go to a steakhouse where they do one thing, but they do that one thing really, really, really well.

They don't offer pasta. They don't offer sushi. They don't offer tacos. They do steak, and that's it. Vegetarians are not going there to eat. They're not trying to be a buffet. It's counterintuitive, but the narrower and the more focused you are, the easier it is to find and book gigs because you know exactly what you're looking for.

One Campaign at a Time

Brandon Birkmeyer: I want to dive into the speaker lab itself. I want to hear how you built it. Was it just booths at conferences the whole time, or did you have a different way to get it going?

Grant Baldwin: We've been bootstrapped from the beginning. First, I created the course. I would also do the webinars. Then, a year or two into it, I had a lot of people asking me to do one-on-one coaching.

I didn't want to do one-on-one coaching. I wanted to build something that was not just dependent on me showing up. Instead, I added a group coaching program, and it was sold over the phone. I did all the sales calls for the first little while.

Eventually, I needed someone to help with sales calls and coaching. For the first several years, it was just a lot of freelance contractors that I would hire. We were about four years into the business before I hired my first true employee.

One thing that we did early on, which is still a big part of what we do to acquire customers, was invest in paid media. We did a lot with Facebook ads and Instagram ads, and today we use TikTok and Google ads and YouTube. For the first several years, we did a lot just on Facebook. That was a big channel for us early on, and it's just a numbers game. If you put a dollar into the Zuckerberg machine, on the other side you can get ten dollars back out.

That was a big part of growth for us and still is to this day. We spend a pretty significant amount on Facebook ads and other forms of paid media every month. There are other channels, like a booth at a conference. That's something we've started experimenting with in the last year.

Eighty to ninety percent of what we sell are core products that we know work. And then we take the ten to twenty percent effort and throw some spaghetti at the wall to see what sticks. We try booths at a conference, affiliate partnerships, and live events. We try different mediums and channels and see what resonates. It all works, but trying to do everything is the thing that doesn't work.

Chapter Fourteen

Lead Your Industry with Progressive Movements

As you move farther down the road on your personal branding journey, you'll be looking for ways to create a greater impact for your audience. After your audience has achieved some quick wins with you and invested in your targeted solutions, they'll be looking for the next step on their journey with you.

That journey starts with you developing your original perspective and beliefs.

Develop Your Original Perspective

The impact you want to have on your audience comes from personally held beliefs about how things should be in your business or industry. Developing those beliefs and your perspective is at the core of maintaining a personal brand long term.

You can start to develop your perspective and beliefs by understanding how they affect the people you are serving. These forces can be positive or negative, but they imply that there's a change happening, and change causes challenges.

Outline all the things happening in your industry, in your world, and around the people you're serving. Think about how the environment around your audience creates challenges for them. As those challenges develop, think of potential solutions, big and small. Come up with singular ideas that would help them quickly and easily solve their problems.

Your job is to help them overcome their challenges. Anyone can come up with ideas to help them solve their problems. Be unique and specific based on your experience and perspective. **There are lots of ways to solve a problem, but your idea is based on the one thing that you think matters the most.**

Pick one thing that can help them find success or solve their problem better than anything else. Share that idea with your people. Lay it out there. That singular belief will inform the series of steps, the order of those steps, and the priority of those steps that people need to take to move forward. But it all starts with a simple perspective.

> If you're having trouble coming up with a perspective, don't worry, it will happen. This is something that develops over time. One great place to start is to ask yourself the question, what is the problem that your audience is up against? And what do you think is the one key to overcoming that problem?

You must focus on one thing, and in the process of choosing that one thing, you'll have to validate that with your own perspective based on your history and ideas. This is how your original perspective starts to form. Original perspective is great because it's an opinion. It's one point of view. It doesn't have to be perfect.

As you choose one perspective and name it as a priority, people can choose to agree or disagree with you. It creates a line in the sand, and people can choose which side of the line they want to stand on.

People who agree with you will join you and be a part of your community to receive the impact of that solution. People who disagree with you will either have a conversation about it and engage in that discussion or decide that someone else has a better solution. And that's okay. Not everybody is going to believe what you believe. Your best customers are the ones who are in alignment with your values and how you think a problem should be solved.

Design Your Progressive Transformation

The second way to lead your industry with progressive movements is to design a progressive transformation. A progressive transformation takes someone from a beginning state to a transformed end state.

You get to decide what that state is based on the problem. You can say that the original state, when they're experiencing a problem, is one thing. And that after they experience the solution, the end state is a different thing. And that new finalized experience should speak to all the wants, beliefs, and desires of your potential audience.

You are not offering impact through random processes. You are offering impact through a journey from one state to a more desirable state. **This transformation should be progressive in nature—it should move them forward from one thing to another, taking them on a journey.**

The more you can focus on what that pain point is and the feeling they will have after that pain point is overcome, the better you'll be able to speak to your audience in a way that helps them understand the impact that you deliver.

Share Signature Ideas and Solutions

The next way you could lead your industry with progressive movements is to share signature ideas and solutions. As you are more developed in sharing your personal brand and creating more impact in the world, the solutions you create start to become longer-term engagements.

As you build signature ideas, your focus should shift to things that continue to help your audience on their journey. This is where you must get creative and identify the next thing your audience will need, again and again.

Sometimes, the steps are cyclical. We might always need a reevaluation or a tune-up of some sort. Those can be signature ideas. Other ideas simply mirror and follow someone on their journey of growth, and you must stay a couple of steps ahead of them along that journey.

What defines a signature idea is that it is not time-based. This idea will work as well today as it will work tomorrow. It does not have an expiration date. Some signature ideas may speak to one step on someone's journey, like the beginning or middle or end.

As you add layers, one at a time, they start to form a cohesive path. The more high-impact signature ideas you can share, the better.

As you look to lead your industry with progressive movements, you are also **transforming yourself from a coach and teacher into a visionary guide and leader**. You get to dream up the future that others can't yet see for themselves.

Activity Break: Set Up Your Leadership Vision

Get started setting up your leadership vision. Here are a few places to start. These worksheets are available at BrandonBirkmeyer/FCL.

Establishing Your Long-Term Goals

- Write down what you want to be known for. Next, write down why you want to be known for that thing and what that helps you accomplish.

- Look down the road five years. Write down your future professional and personal goals. Get specific.

  - Professional - List what job and position you want, what type of work you want to do, and who you want to work with. Write down what skills you want to have developed and what experiences you will have gained.

  - Personal - List what type of lifestyle you want. Write down what you want your home life to look like. List your values and what success looks like.

Creating a Vision Board

- Once per year, find words, images, and objects that represent your vision of the future.

- Create a visual representation of that vision. You can create a vision board physically or digitally. Keep that vision board in a place that you can see it every day.

Setting Up Your Milestones

- Look at your five-year vision and write down the milestones you'd have to achieve to reach it. Divide your milestones across a five-year window and create annual goals to hit those milestones.

- Divide your annual goals into monthly milestones, and write down what you need to accomplish to reach those goals.

- Write down daily and weekly projects/priorities that will help you reach your monthly goals.

Tracking Your Progress

- Each quarter, review your progress toward your goals. Write down your wins and your challenges. Celebrate your wins and come up with a plan to overcome your challenges.

- Consider finding or creating an accountability group. Share your journey with other people, and get encouragement and support along the way.

Interview with Stan Phelps
IG: STANPHELPSSPEAKS

Stan Phelps is a *Forbes* contributor, TEDx speaker, IBM Futurist, Certified Speaking Professional, and best-selling author of the Goldfish series of business books, including *Purple Goldfish – 10 Ways to Attract Raving Customers*. He is also an instructor for the ANA School of Marketing and Rutgers Business School and is a great example of leading an industry with progressive movements.

Stan's Goldfish series of business books focus on the little ways to drive differentiation, increase loyalty, and promote positive word of mouth. They cover a range of topics, including customer experience, employee engagement, differentiation, technology/data/analytics, key stakeholders, passion/purpose, happiness/productivity, generational differences, sales, presentations, and differentiated experiences.

Build One Small Step at a Time

Brandon Birkmeyer: What came first, the books or the professional speaking? How did it go, and what worked for you?

Stan Phelps: I don't think you need to have a book if you want to be a speaker. However, I'm all about differentiation. The fact that you have a book on the topic that you speak about is a huge differentiator. Now, should it be a differentiator? That's debatable. But it certainly is a proof point of your commitment to that topic, and specifically your take on that topic.

Since I was around twenty years old, I have had a goal to write a book at some point in my life. I'm not alone; the research shows that about eight percent of Americans, when asked that question, think they've got a book in them. But how many of them get it done? Just about one percent.

In the beginning, I never thought it would be a series. Once you start to go far enough down a road on something, your perspective and thinking changes.

My first book, *Purple Goldfish*, was all about winning customers. I studied over a thousand examples, and I realized something. The companies that truly understood how to win customers did not put the customer first; they put their employees first.

I had to explore what these companies were doing to create a great workplace where you are reinforcing culture and have engaged employees. So, my second book, *Green Goldfish*, was about employee engagement. In this book, I had another aha moment that led to my third book. And then, so on and so forth, with more books. It's been a journey.

Last year, it was fun to write *Black Goldfish*—chronicling the journey of how my understanding has changed over a decade.

And now, the next decade is more about creating impact and less about thought leadership. I've created a vehicle for that called The Goldfish Tank, which combines a keynote or workshop and a little bit of personalized coaching to get people to come up with impactful ideas and implementable ideas.

The next decade for me is getting people to create that impact.

Brandon Birkmeyer: How do you decide the amount of research that goes into your books?

Stan Phelps: I enjoy the research process. For the first two books, I did over a thousand crowdsourced examples. Now, I find that two to four hundred examples are about all you need because things become repetitive. I love trying to see the patterns that develop and how I can create a framework around my research findings. It's become a repeatable process.

I also realized that, for a lot of the areas that I wanted to go into, I wasn't the expert. I wrote the first three books on my own. For the remaining books in the series, I've had coauthors. They bring the subject matter expertise that I don't have. Plus, it helps share the lift of doing the research, analysis, and writing.

Explore the Many Paths to Your Future

Brandon Birkmeyer: How does having so many books help or potentially hurt your business?

Stan Phelps: I'm the antithesis of whatever advice I would give to anyone who was thinking about following a similar path because I would tell you to focus on one thing. Focus on one industry and go deep on that one thing.

There's somebody I know who just does work within construction management. I've never spoken at any event in that industry, but this is the go-to person for that industry. And it's because they've developed stuff around every aspect within that vertical, and they probably do four times as much speaking as I do.

I don't know if having excessive books hurts me. I love the variety of the organizations that I speak for. I was just having a conversation today with somebody in higher education. Later this afternoon, I'm having a conversation with a law firm. Two weeks ago, I was working with someone in the pharmaceutical and medical device space. The week before that, I was with a grocers' association. I love the variety, but I wouldn't recommend it to anyone else.

Listen to the full interviews and BrandonBirkmeyer.com/FCL.

Chapter Fifteen

Actions That Matter – Escaping the Sea of Sameness

P ersonal branding requires you to take action. In your professional life, you are a product competing for attention. And just like with a product, attention is hard to win.

In the world of business, there are so many products and so many messages flooding the market. In marketing, the goal is to break through the clutter. That clutter is often called the "sea of sameness."

We are all taking in thousands of messages every day. We have ads that are constantly being shown to us across different media types. On television, radio, and the internet, on our phones and social media, and everywhere else we go, we're exposed to more and more messages. Meanwhile, our attention spans are getting shorter and shorter.

The average attention span on social media is under ten seconds. That's very short. You have a small window of time to capture someone's attention, hook them, engage with them, and hopefully drive some type of call to action.

The sea of sameness never ends. It only grows. There are more and more ads, messages, and businesses every day adding to the clutter.

It's not just businesses that are pulled into the sea of sameness. Human beings are also competing to get attention. A competitive workforce often leads to saturation and pulls you into a sea of sameness. Put plainly, there are lots of humans that do the things that you do. **You are always in competition for resources, jobs, clients, and attention.**

In the workforce, people are products. When companies are looking to fill a position or solve a problem, **you are one of many options that the business can choose to do that job** and solve that problem. When you are running your own business, you are one of many businesses that can solve the same problem.

To get ahead, you must escape that sea of sameness. To stand out from the competition, grab the attention of your target audience and make yourself more noticeable—more discoverable, more memorable. Eventually, you'll be chosen by the audience.

As you start to look more closely at your own reputation, look for opportunities to stand out when and where you are being compared to others. That starts with looking at your past experience.

Be More than a Resume

Your reputation and relationships are more likely to get you a job or a client than your resume. Most people focus on their resumes and ignore the rest.

Your resume is one of the first things you share as a potential job candidate. It must filter through different barriers of attention before finally reaching the end decision-maker. That's just the beginning of the process of getting a job and keeping it, much less climbing the ranks.

Some people don't even make it through that clutter to the first opportunity. In fact, many jobs, if not *most* jobs these days, don't even take the resumes generally submitted for the job into consideration. **They look at relationships, recommendations, and referrals to fill positions first.**

With digital job postings, it is easier for people to find listings and apply for jobs. You're competing with more people than ever at this initial phase of the process. So, it's important to know what's in your resume and how you are getting it in front of people. Relevant work history, high-profile clients, and specialized skills aren't enough to guarantee you a job because there are lots of people who fit those criteria.

The question is not just what's in your resume, but **who do you know that can give the resume to the right person**. When you manage to get through the gatekeepers, they need to know that you meet the minimum requirements and are employable. However, relationships are more important than the resume in the beginning. It's better to have an internal person at the organization that you've networked with who can recommend you or refer you.

One of the most important things you can do is be out there, building your reputation with other people. Build your network so that you know more people in the organizations that are hiring people like you. You must be highly networked in the industry that will hire you.

And these days, even that's not enough. As you progress through an organization and move up the ranks step-by-step, there are fewer and fewer jobs toward the top of the organization. Even if there are ten positions at the bottom of a particular business, the people in those ten positions are typically fighting for five or fewer positions above that and then one or two positions above that. It's a giant funnel.

You are consistently being forced to compete, not just because of your resume but because of the competition within the hierarchy of your organization. Trying to shine within the organization itself is not easy. Even after you're hired and employed, you are still in the sea of sameness.

When you have a job, you must continue to expand your resume while growing your network. You want to be more employable in case you lose the job or get stuck without opportunities for growth. You must also build your reputation internally in the organization.

Start by thinking about how your reputation looks from an outsider's perspective. Know what people say when they start to talk about you. The actions you take and the things you do are memorable. You are being watched and measured just as much as you are watching and measuring. The things you accomplish, the projects you take on, the way you show up—all these things are considered when people you interact with eventually have to make a referral or a recommendation.

Everyone has their opinions of you and, yes, they matter. In addition to your boss and your clients, this includes peers, coworkers, vendors, and even people in the industry.

Don't underestimate the power of the people who work directly at your level. At some point, as you all matriculate through different companies, those former coworkers may be the people who let you know that a job opportunity exists at the next company that they move to, and they're looking for someone like you. If they had a great relationship with you, they may bring you in as a referral for that next job.

It's more than just your resume. It's more than your relationships and reputation. Now, we also have the internet. People will Google you. You need to know what people will find when they look you up.

Be More than a Referral

After the referral gets your foot in the door, your online presence tells your unique story. Most people do the bare minimum, but it takes more than that to stand out.

Say someone mentions your name and says, "Hey, this person is great. I had a good experience with them. You should check them out."

The natural next step would be to not only look at your resume, if they have it, but also to look for you online. **People will search for as much information as they can find about you.**

Just as you must nurture the relationships with the people who could be referrals for you, **you have to nurture your online identity so that when people search for you, they find something worth seeing**. And the first thing people typically find is your social media presence and, specifically, your professional presence on a site like LinkedIn. You need to be there.

This is one that often gets overlooked. A lot of the time, you just repost your resume information onto your LinkedIn profile and your social profiles and stop there. But everyone does that. Sharing your ideas online and creating content is how you stand out online. And there are lots of ways to create content and share ideas online.

Be More than a LinkedIn Profile

When building an online presence, quality matters. Before people get to know you, the only thing they have to judge you by is the image you've presented.

Think about what people find when they Google you. **Most social media was built to be social, not professional.** It's okay for social posts to be findable online. But they must be curated in a way that lifts you up rather than drags you down. We have all heard of someone who has lost an opportunity because of a picture that made them look less than professional or not aligned with the company culture of a potential employer. Many times, they don't even know it. They just know they aren't getting calls back.

Typically, potential employers will get a sense of your ideas, your attitude and behavior, and your personality, as well as a general feeling and image from the things that are being shown. For example, if you post content that is business-related, but every time you do it, it's in front of a messy desk, you could be judged. If you post while on a walk or while you're exercising and you look sweaty, you could be judged. That's the image they'll get versus your competition, which may be more professional.

You are being compared to content that looks great from an office, or in front of bookshelves, or in some other curated environment with higher-quality video and sound and better lighting. All of that can be judged and compared, and it may influence a decision-maker who is, at the end of the day, human and biased.

Think about the clothes you wear in pictures and videos. Think about what's happening in the background of your content. Take into consideration everything that can be seen and heard. The more you can do to manage the environment, the more you're doing to manage your personal brand. Everything they see gets counted and is attached to the brand that you're building, even if it's unintentional. **If they have an opportunity to see it, it has an opportunity to be a part of your reputation and your personal brand.**

Just as important, you need to be able to be found by people who aren't looking for you.

Be More than a Google Result

Thought leadership proves your authority and influence. Many people have lots to say about themselves, but you'll stand out more when other people are talking about you and your ideas.

This is a big one that a lot of people underestimate. If someone's looking for a particular answer to a question or a particular type of person and they search in a directory, you want to show up rather than someone else.

A good example of this is a blog article. If you wrote a blog article on a popular topic in your industry and that article is on your website and it gets indexed by Google search, you are more likely to appear in the search results. If someone types that "how to" question into Google and your content is the result, you have a chance to build credibility.

Your high-ranking blog post on a particular topic helps position you as a leader on that topic to people in your industry. Another great way to build authority is to have your content and ideas featured on someone else's media channel. If you have a featured article in a top publication or you were a guest on a big show or podcast in your industry, it creates social proof for your expertise which helps your reputation.

It separates you as someone who has positioned themselves as a knowledge-able professional versus someone who barely has a presence online or someone who just submitted a resume.

PART 3

The Four Laws of Front & Center Leadership

Chapter Sixteen

What's Stopping You – The Paradox of Routine

How many decisions do you make every day, whether conscious or unconscious, and why do you make those decisions? A lot of the decisions you make are inconsequential to the outcomes of your daily life. Things as simple as where you sit in the movie theater when you go to watch a movie, what restaurant you are going to eat at, or what you are going to make yourself for lunch are seemingly innocuous decisions.

When you start to examine these decisions, they can become pretty interesting in terms of explaining who you are as a person, or at least how you make decisions. It's fun to look at some of those patterns to figure out how you behave and some tweaks you can make that might improve your life. We all have routines programmed into our lives.

For example, one of my routines kicks in when I go to the movie theater. I go to the same theater and sit in the same seats every time. It's a pattern that I've developed, and maybe some of you can relate. I know that if I go to a movie theater, the first three rows are always going to be the worst because I am buried under the movie screen, and I have to crank my head all the way back the entire movie. It's going to be uncomfortable. Whereas the second section that's raised up, typically about the third row deep, is where I'm just far enough away to see the whole screen comfortably every time. And that's where I prefer to find seats.

That's my routine. I've consciously decided, over time, where I like to sit. And now I don't even think about it. I don't stray from that decision.

There are other decisions that I'll go with the flow on. There are times when I'm okay doing what everyone else wants to do. I don't really care. If we're going out to a restaurant or making weekend plans, I'm happy to go with the flow because I'll have fun wherever we are. Those aren't important decisions to me.

As I started to look at these routine behaviors, I started thinking about routines in our professional lives. Specifically, **I wanted to know how our routines affect the decisions we make.** Whether you are someone in the workforce, an entrepreneur, an executive, or anyone else, you are confronted with decisions of varying levels of importance. You tend to handle those decisions in one of four ways:

- The conscious routine decision

- The unconscious decision

- The indecisive decision

- The decisive decision

The Conscious Routine Decision

The easiest decisions you make are the decisions you make every day, repeating decisions based on past experience. You already know the outcome of these decisions. They are easy and safe. But they are also routine and boring. I call this the paradox of routine.

The paradox of routine suggests we are generally happier, less stressed people when we make routine decisions. Routines help us, but they can be boring and sometimes limiting. They are natural ways that our minds and bodies work to create order and reduce stress in our lives.

I know that when I have a routine, I'm a happier person. If I know when I'm going to wake up, where I have to go, what I'm going to eat, and what my day is going to look like, I'm a happier person.

I can eat a peanut butter and jelly sandwich every day for lunch for the rest of my life and be totally fine. There's certainty in that I know what to expect. I know how much work it takes. I'm going to get what I need, and I'll get through it in a timely way where I can get back to work. It's quick. It's easy. And I know that I'm going to enjoy it (even if it's a little boring).

Routines are easy, but they can become repetitive and redundant. There's not a lot of innovation or invention that happens when you're in a routine. And that's the point of it, but it can lead to some dissatisfaction if you are growing bored with that routine.

Now, in the case of lunch, it's easy to change it up every now and then. But for bigger decisions, change can be more difficult. Routines can be helpful, or they can be harmful.

In a career, for example, there's a lot of day-to-day work that becomes routine. It's built that way. Companies use systems that make it easier to run the business, bring in new employees, and transition them through the organization. Jobs are set up so that anyone who has the right set of qualifications can do them. But **if it's easy, anyone can do it, and you are replaceable**. That leads to what I call the commoditization of human work—a very real thing.

For example, if you move into a corporate environment, you have the security of that type of job path. But the job that you are learning is the same job, with the same methods, that the person before you did—and the person before them, and the person before them, and so on. There's a set way to do things, with no innovation going on. It's menial work because it's been designed that way to get you started.

It's essentially an assembly line, and it gets boring because you're doing repetitive tasks. You stay because you hope to grow and be trained in the next position above that. But this happens again and again, in every position. You're just taking on slightly newer, more complex assembly-line work.

It goes from basic assistant work, to slightly more interesting executional work, to more tactical decision-making. Then you jump to more strategic decision-making at the management level and to client interaction at the higher leadership levels. Then, eventually, you may move to executive-level operations and business development and executive leadership and management, etc.

It's an organized structure and system, and it's been perfected by big organizations. Systems are designed to create efficient organizations, manage teams, and support leadership. **The system that creates stability, happiness, and lower stress is also the system that creates boredom and a lack of innovation.**

It's why some of the biggest companies are at the biggest risk of being taken over or surpassed by faster, younger startups that are innovating in the space; a company that has less red tape and fewer routines. In those cases, the paradox of routine can be a problem.

The conscious decisions you're making can be a problem. Your normal routine and patterns can be a problem. If you're someone within the organization, you as an individual have those same types of routines. You have a normal way that you perform at your job or that you look to be evaluated for that performance. You have a normal way of showing up, arriving, and participating in meetings, of engaging in projects, and of accomplishing the work that you're given.

For someone looking to grow in an organization, you can explore those routines to see if they are benefiting you. You can **ask yourself if there are different ways to operate**. And that conscious decision is what's going to start to separate you from the rest of the crowd that's following the same routine.

Someone may have a great resume, but it's hard to know whether they are going to be good until they get into the routine of the project and then fit in or don't fit in. When it's time to decide who is to going to be promoted from within the team, they look for anyone who stands out and those that align best with the values of the organization.

It's those little nuances that move you toward being promoted more quickly versus following the standard timeline of waiting and waiting for your turn. You get to make the conscious decision and choose if you want to wait on someone else or to act toward your goals.

The Unconscious Decision

Some of your decisions, in fact, most of the decisions that you make every day, are unconscious decisions.

It's staggering to think about the amount of your life that is happening on autopilot. A lot of the choices you make early in your life are programmed into your subconscious as a routine. You make those decisions automatically and do things the same way over and over again. Your decisions are based on innate feelings, instincts, and thoughts that you have based on pattern recognition.

It feels like a gut decision, but it's actually based on things that you've built routines around over time. You've already decided how you feel and how you would act in certain situations.

Do you remember how much memorization we had to do as kids? I have a son who is in first grade, and he has homework with a lot of memorization. When he's learning math, they have games where he's trying to quickly answer very simple math problems. If they say, "two plus two," he immediately answers, "four," because that's the answer embedded in his subconscious through rote learning. He didn't have to do math and count one, two, three, four. Those types of memories are programmed into your subconscious so that it's just known.

Memorization helps you get through things more quickly and saves energy, so you can move on to higher-level problems. It's fun to watch it happen as it develops. At first, as a kid, you wonder how you will possibly remember all these things. But through practice and repetition, it happens. And that's how it goes for everyone. You learn the flow of something, it gets programmed in, and then you don't think about it anymore.

That makes it easy to fall into routines that are there to make your life easier. There are routines individualized to you, and there are routines that are more social, affecting groups of people. The point is, you have your patterns.

Whether they're created by the environment or by your own choices, those natural patterns become unconscious, and that's just how you act.

It's interesting to look at some of the decisions you make and actions you take and to ask yourself if this is how you want to act and think moving forward. Just that simple act of observing the situation allows you to take it from being an unconscious decision to a conscious decision. You have the power to decide if it's a decision you actually want to make.

> This is important, especially in the corporate environment, where a lot of your actions can become unconscious and are based on what you see in the environment. A lot of your opportunities to stand out and get ahead are going to be created by taking different courses of action than the norm. But you must be observant about the environment and make decisions to do things that move you forward.

You can find opportunities to do things that go above and beyond. You can take ownership of projects. You can explore and be curious about things, asking the extra questions. You can get a new person involved in the decision to bring in different insights. You can come up with original ideas and improve on old ideas. The key to all of this is taking the time to be observant and aware.

The Indecisive Decision

There are times when you find yourself in a situation where you are not sure what to do. You can see that there's a decision ahead of you, but the course of action is not obvious. You just let others decide because there's a lot of pros and cons. Sometimes, it seems like other people have a strong inclination toward or preference for one thing, so you go with it.

You assume that if they're feeling this strongly about it, they probably have a better reason than yours. In fact, it's been observed that if there's an expert on something in the room, you tend to default to what that person says, and your ability to think about and analyze a problem diminishes. You would just rely on the expert. This is called the uncertainty principle.

The uncertainty principle says that when you are not sure about a decision, when you don't have enough information, or if you have too much information, you'll generally default to other people. You'll go with the flow. And that can be dangerous in a lot of situations. Defaulting to what others say is never going to help you get ahead.

The Decisive Decision

What it takes to be decisive is a little bit of preparation. To be certain in a situation means that you might have to do a little work ahead of time so that you either understand the situation better or you understand yourself and your own preferences better. What it takes to be confident in a decision is to either know as many details about the situation as you can or how you make decisions based on a limited number of details.

Decisiveness comes from understanding your values and principles and doing the research on the situation. Decisiveness comes from the confidence you have in knowing what you are talking about.

If you know a decision is coming and you want to be decisive, do the research ahead of time. Be the person who over-prepares and asks questions so they can go behind the scenes and develop an opinion or a perspective on the situation. You can practice having opinions and a perspective. "Well, generally I think this, this, and this in this situation because of X, Y, and Z."

With preparation, you can understand your values better. You can understand what things matter to you the most in business, life, and work situations. Write them down, and challenge yourself to think about them. If someone asked you why you would make the decision you shared, you could explain your values to them. For example, you value speed, or you value simplicity, or you value people. Figure out the important criteria, and use them to help you make those decisions. **Understanding your own values and doing a little bit of preparation ahead of time helps to unlock and move you forward.**

Chapter Seventeen

LAW #1 Step Up for the Right Reasons

L eadership is a choice. When you choose to do more than others are willing to do, you are choosing leadership. Leadership is hard because it requires you to be better than average. You are choosing the more challenging road because you want a better-than-average result. This only works when your intention aligns with your effort.

Most people don't want to make the effort. Welcome to the Stagnation Nation!

The Stagnation Nation are the people who are stuck at one point or another in their lives. It's natural for us to hit a limit in our capabilities or progress as humans. Getting stuck happens.

The question is, where are you stuck? And are you motivated to get unstuck? The choices you make will determine where you excel and where you fail.

Find Your Motivation

The truth is, we are all creatures of comfort. If we don't have to push ourselves, we tend not to push ourselves. If we can't find the motivation to make an effort, we won't. So, how do people who are naturally stagnant find the drive and motivation to get unstuck?

The question ends up being a very personal one. It's different for everyone. Some people are in survival mode. Their motivations go as far as what it takes to put food on the table, keep their kids healthy, pay their bills, and stay alive.

If you can find the energy to move beyond survival mode, you need to be careful where you put that valuable energy. This is where goal-setting comes in.

Goal-setting is easier in an established environment than in something new. It helps if you can find motivation to push yourself a little further in your current job or business. But it's not as obvious in some jobs or paths as others. In sports, for example, it's simple. You want to beat the other team. You figure out what you must do to beat the other team. **You decide the skills that you must work on. Then you put in the work.**

You decide how much exercise and training you need. You analyze the competition for strengths and weaknesses. You learn what it's going to take to beat them. In this type of situation, the answers are obvious and specific.

In your career, it can be a little less obvious. It's hard to know what to practice and what to get better at to push yourself past other people.

> Most people are waiting for others to tell them what to do to get unstuck. They wait to be told the specific areas where they could perform better. They wait for their annual review to tell them the three things that they can be working on over the next twelve months to get slightly better at their job. But not you! You are ready to push beyond average.

The problem with performance reviews is that they're very generic. And they may highlight one or two things that you did all year. Your areas of improvement may not actually help develop you and push you ahead of other people. Average feedback is, at best, going to lead to an average performance.

You may become slightly more communicative or slightly more strategic or slightly more poised at presentations, but none of these things are really going to set you apart from other people.

Find Your Destination

To push yourself and get unstuck, you need to have a specific goal and purposeful practice to push beyond what is ordinary. Anyone can get good at presenting something or solving a problem, but how dc you get great at something? Start by being more specific. **When you have a specific goal that you are motivated toward, stagnation falls aside.**

If you want to get better at something, :ry purposeful practice. Purposeful practice is an exercise where you determine a limit and then work to break that limit incrementally over time. It's been tested and proven that purposeful practice can help you push beyond your natural limits.

For example, there are people out there who can memorize very long sets of numbers, and this is abnormal. When given a string of numbers straight and then asked to recite them back, the average person can remember maybe eight or nine at most.

But then researchers tested purposeful practice, each time challenging people to go one number higher. If they made a mistake, they'd go back one or two steps and try again. As they started to get it right they'd be given one number higher and repeat the process over and over again. Incrementally adding challenges one step at a time made the difference. Purposeful practice broke the limits of their performance.

Find a goal that you can be purposefully practicing, pushing just beyond your limit. Prove to yourself that you can consistently go beyond that limit. And then push that limit again. Break out of the ordinary and become extraordinary.

How often do we actually do this? Not many of us practice something so much that we are extraordinary.

This means not just learning and reading; it means executing something and then getting feedback on it. And then, based on that feedback, trying again, and trying to improve. That feedback must continually push you slightly out of your comfort zone so that you can move forward.

Find Your Determination

Any basketball fans that followed Kobe Bryant know about what Kobe called the "black mamba mentality." This mentality is about attacking what's in front of you with full focus and determination. Kobe had a reputation of being the first person to arrive and the last to leave at practices and games.

He would be consistently working on the same basketball moves over and over again. The moves became so ingrained in his body that they were automatic. But not everyone had that same work ethic. Not everyone was willing to put in that same effort, to try that same thing.

The other undercover advantage was that when the competition noticed that someone was working that hard at something, it was so intimidating that they'd back off.

There's a psychological game that's happening around us, whether we know it or not. In our lives, businesses, and at work, we are in competition. At work, **people recognize the extraordinary**. When you're the one putting in the work and people notice, they typically let you take a leadership role.

If you want more opportunities to win, become the person who puts in the work that gets noticed. Be the one that is practicing the hardest. Learn the skills that stand out in an organization, business, or company. Take on a "black mamba mentality."

End of Chapter Questions

Get your worksheet for this chapter at BrandonBirkmeyer.com/FCL.

- Reflect on your current role and career trajectory. Are there areas where you feel stuck or stagnant in your professional growth? Describe these areas and consider what might be holding you back.

- Think about the skills and competencies required for success in your field. Which of these skills do you feel are your weakest areas? How can you prioritize these skills for improvement?

- Consider the concept of purposeful practice in skill development. What specific skills do you want to focus on improving, and how can you incorporate purposeful practice into your daily routine to enhance these skills?

- Reflect on past experiences of pushing beyond your comfort zone and achieving success. How can you harness these experiences to cultivate determination and resilience in your pursuit of skill development?

- Explore the resources and support systems available to you for skill development. Who can you turn to for guidance, mentorship, or feedback as you work to improve your skills?

- Assess your current level of commitment to professional growth. What obstacles or challenges are standing in the way of your progress, and how can you overcome them?

Chapter Eighteen

LAW #2 Step Up with the Right Message

You can do all the work in the word to put your message in front of people and introduce yourself and your brand, but if the creative and the messaging are wrong, people either won't know it's for them or they won't see the value.

Your message is everything. Sometimes, the creative message is accurate but not interesting. Sometimes, the message is interesting but not valuable. There are many nuances to what makes creative messaging work effectively.

There's even more work to be done on messaging for a personal brand. Your creative is tied to you, your ideas, and your message. The best step forward is to look at the formats you're choosing for your message and then learn the best practices of those formats. If you are a YouTuber, you must learn the best creative practices for YouTube. If you are a podcaster, learn the best practices and formats of engaging podcasts. It's the same with social media. Look at what types of posts are trending now or are popular. Look at what's working and getting people's attention. You must become a student of the media channels that you are creating on.

Not only should you be following the best practices of your media channels but also for your packaging. Your message is affected by your packaging. Look at a brand like Coca-Cola. The promotion is one piece of the message, but the packaging of the product itself is another branding element with multiple formats to choose from.

You, yourself, as a personal brand, also have packaging. It's the words you're saying, and it's the things people see and hear.

You are being compared to other messaging that people are seeing on the media channels. If you want to be found, chosen, and seen, the message and packaging must be interesting enough for people to pick you over someone else. How you present yourself matters.

What Should You Create?

Your message is also molded by the format of what you're creating. For most personal brands, if you are just getting started, there are a couple of ways to get the ball rolling.

As you embark on this creative journey, you must:

- think like a creator – Is your message crystal clear?

- act like a showman – Is your message connecting with your audience?

- package your ideas – Is your message aligned with the context of where you are sharing it?

Think Like a Creator

The most important thing about creative messaging is that it is clear and focused on a message that makes sense for the creator themself.

You may have lots of interests. Those interests can span a variety of categories and industries. **Your personal brand, however, should not start as a variety show** that talks about everything. A variety show is not an interesting format for a personal brand unless you are already a celebrity. You must boil down your interests to the things you want to be known for.

> Clarity will come for some people right away. For others, it will come through action. Start creating content about things that you like to talk about every day, and then look backwards to find the themes. Look for the pattern of things that you like to talk about over and over. Start to focus on just those things, and cut it down to the ones that are most important for what you want to be known for.

Clarity is going to come with time and focus. When you start thinking like a creator, it empowers you to create with confidence. Put things out there that you're proud of and like to talk about. Stick to topics that you know. If you talk about things that you are unsure about or are unfamiliar with, you will lose confidence. That lack of confidence will negatively affect your performance.

Anything that you can talk about for hours, off the top of your head, is a perfect topic for you. Yes, you can expand beyond that eventually as you are developing new skills. However, in the moment of creation, focus on talking about things that you already know.

One option is to find a fact, statistic, or trend and then react to it. That way, you're just memorizing one thing and not everything. And your reactions will be based on your experiences—they will come from you. They won't just be regurgitations of some facts you found online.

Don't lose sight of constancy. Constancy is the quality of being enduring and unchanging. It's different than consistency. Consistency is about sticking to a set of rules. As a content creator, consistency is when you set a schedule and you stick to it so that you meet people's expectations. This is important, but a bigger priority for a personal brand is being a constant figure in the eyes of your audience.

Constancy, for your personal brand, means that you are always around and always showing up. As a creator, you need to be ever-present. An audience, once you've established a following, expects regular access to you or your ideas. If you aren't constantly showing up, they'll find somewhere else to go.

If you're a creator, you're thinking of your audience first. It means you've made a promise to show up consistently, yes, but more importantly, you are constantly present. There's always something there from you that they can find.

Act Like a Showman

When you start presenting things and sharing your ideas more often, the way you present them becomes important. It's not about you anymore. The goal of your presentations is to give your people what they want to hear. Connect with them. Make them feel something.

A showman knows that keeping someone's attention is infinitely important. Bring some showmanship into your ideas. For example, try different formats—make your show shorter or longer. Bring in guests or create some other variety when you are giving a speech. Try to design a performance so that it is entertaining and keeps the attention of an audience.

You can act like a showman in all your thought leadership work and content and when networking and relationship building. Just remember, **the goal is to engage your audience**. The focus isn't on you; it's on them. Even if you are the star of the show, it's in the service of the audience. Show up in a way that entertains or engages and is memorable. If they are engaged and remember you, they will tell other people about you.

Package Your Ideas

The final component of messaging is packaging your ideas. Your ideas need to be put together in a way that allows people to understand them and become interested in them.

Every time you share a perspective, people need to understand how to use it. **A message without context is confusing.** When crafting your story, think about how you introduce it, how you tell it, and how you conclude it. And make sure the story is relevant to the audience. Stories are great, but they need structure and purpose. Don't fall into the trap of creating random content and telling long stories that have no message.

Another mistake is to have too many messages. Don't wrap your message in clutter. When you overload people with content and stories, it can be hard to follow. When packaging your ideas, the message should be singular, clear, and obvious from the start. Storytelling is hugely important, but it must have a purpose.

The other piece to packaging your ideas is how you present things. **Your packaging includes how you look, how you sound, and the ideas that you talk about.** All the stories you include, the industry reports, and anything you create or build must be packaged in a way that is clear and engaging. Your audience should be happy to continue to lean in and hear more.

If you provide an industry report that is all text with no charts, no graphs, and no design, fewer people will be motivated to read it. Even if the information is infinitely valuable. Adding some design elements that take into consideration how people consume the content is always important. If you're at an in-person event where you are giving some type of presentation, consider how long the presentation is and what will work best in that amount of time. Think about the audience and when they need breaks Only keep what's critical to include, and remove the rest.

One piece of content can be delivered in many ways. A fifteen-minute idea can be delivered very differently than a one-hour idea or a half-minute idea, even if it's the same idea. Packaging your ideas is critical to making sure that your message resonates in a way that helps you stand out from the competition.

End of Chapter Questions

Get your worksheet for this chapter at BrandonBirkmeyer.com/FCL.

- What are the key topics or themes that resonate with you the most?

- How can you tailor your content delivery to make it more entertaining and memorable?

- What are some creative ways to incorporate variety and excitement into your content or presentations?

- How can you ensure that your content is visually appealing and easy to consume?

- Consider a presentation or report you've created in the past. How could you improve its packaging to better resonate with your audience?

- What steps will you take to refine your message packaging strategy moving forward?

Chapter Nineteen

LAW #3 Stand Out in the Right Places

V isibility is one of the most important factors in terms of standing out. It's the opportunity for people to see you—whether as a person, a product, a business, or an advertisement. When people can't see what you are selling, they don't buy it, and if people can't see you, they don't know you.

A lot of people worry about things like the frequency of contact and the number of times you interact with your customers, or the frequency of hearing something or seeing something, but visibility is more important. For example, if you are selling something, you have a better chance of selling it by asking ten people one time than you do if you ask one person ten times.

Yes, it's true that, in advertising, it helps to get people to see your ad more than once, but reaching more people is still the priority.

I'm not saying you should try reaching everyone, just everyone right for you. More visibility with the right people is the goal.

Visibility is critical to personal branding. If you want to stand out, your job is to get in front of and be visible to as many people as possible and to make a good impression. Not just any people; the right people.

Yes, eventually, a secondary goal is to then deepen the relationship by getting in front of them again. But in the beginning, the priority must be to reach as many of the right people as possible.

There are some factors that you can control that contribute to visibility:

- Reach – How many people know about you?

- Discoverability – Are people able to find you?

- Distribution – Do you show up where people spend time?

Broaden Your Reach

Reach is the ability for you to deliver your message, your product, or yourself to as many people as possible. Reach can be created in many ways.

The easiest thing to do is to get yourself in front of more people. As a personal brand, to create reach, you can either meet people in person or virtually. You could reach them one-on-one, by meeting them in person and shaking their hand. Or you could meet them virtually, through content marketing or paid advertising.

Many people build their personal brand in person. **The way to capitalize on reach in person is to go to places where there are more of the right people that you want to meet.**

For example, let's say you go to a small networking group of thirty people for two hours. If ten of them are the right people for you to meet, you have a chance to meet all ten. You shake their hands. They get to know you. You now have visibility amongst those ten people.

However, in that same one hour of time, if you were at a larger conference with three hundred people, your reach goes up. You can meet hundreds of people in that same amount of time, all in person. You would shake more hands, make more introductions, and have more conversations. You may even make friends that introduce you to other people.

What if you have a booth at a conference? Now you're a destination, where people gather, walk by, look, and observe, seeing you based on your position at that conference. You can even hire people to work at the booth for you!

What if you were speaking on stage at that conference? Instead of speaking to each person one at a time, you are speaking to many people all at once. Now your reach is even higher. If you're giving a speech to a hundred people at a conference, every one of them is looking at you on the stage and getting to know you better in your zone of genius.

In each of these cases, your reach and visibility go up. Your reach is based on the opportunity to be in front of the right people and how many people you can talk to at the same time, but **there are a lot of limits to in-person reach, which is why content marketing has become popular**.

Content marketing is different than paid advertising. Content marketing is creating your own content and putting it somewhere it can be found at no cost to you. That could be content that lives in a blog, on a YouTube channel, on a podcast, on a website, or on social media. Anything you create that is yours, that you post for people to find, is content marketing.

You can place and promote content marketing on channels that you create and own or on other free channels, such as social media. The problem with social media or any channel that someone else owns is that you are reliant on the power of their distribution to deliver your message to their audiences.

The other problem with social media is you're competing with a lot of other people and their messages. You're trying to find the eyeballs of the right people to reach, but you don't control who you reach. You are at the mercy of social media distribution.

In some cases, it could be very generous. In other cases, it might not be so generous. Generally, when a social media channel is new, and there are more people watching than creating, you might have an advantage. That's why so many new social media channels create audiences faster than channels that have become saturated with creators.

The other type of reach comes from paid advertising. **Once you have a budget and some money to invest, advertising is the fastest way to gain reach.** The reason it's the fastest is that you are using social media channels that have already built audiences to force distribution to the audiences that you choose, and that's going to cost you money. The effectiveness of that reach will depend on the strength of your message and the accuracy of the campaign to reach the right people.

Paid advertising has been one of the strongest tools for large businesses to reach people. And now, with advertising such as online digital marketing becoming easier to use, individuals have access to grow their audience. Anyone can create an ad online. You can pay to reach the right people at a reasonable cost, and you can test that over time. You can build it, optimize it, and start to scale it as things get more efficient.

This too, however, is a competitive space. As more access is provided, it creates more competition and raises advertising prices. But at the end of the day, reach is the only way to grow visibility. And visibility is the fastest way to stand out.

Increase Your Discoverability

Not only do you need to push your message in front of a lot of people, but people also need to be able to discover that message on their own.

Discoverability means creating things in a targeted way so that when people are looking for them, they can find them. Findable means that you are organizing it in a way that aligns with where people are and how they search.

If you put your message on a piece of paper and print a million copies of it but you drop those million copies in the middle of a desert, no one will see it. Just like there are TV shows airing at three in the morning, when almost no one is watching, and there are websites on the internet that no one has ever visited. Your message must be discoverable.

If you go to a conference to meet people but all you do is sit and watch the speakers speak, and you don't introduce yourself to anyone, you'll do zero work to help your visibility. You must be discoverable, and maybe people will come to you for that reason. You can sit or stand in the right place or join people at a table. You can stand in a line where there are other people standing or wear an outfit that brings people to you to make a comment on it and start a conversation. All of that is discoverability.

The other thing about being discoverable is that it must be targeted toward someone. If you are trying to reach everyone, then typically, you're reaching no one because there's no reason for them to find you. People generally like to group together based on common interests or based on some type of specific factor that brings them to you. Sometimes, they are looking for an answer to a problem that they're trying to solve, they're trying to meet certain types of people, or they are participating in certain types of groups.

We've mentioned findability in terms of keywords and copy, but it also means that you are putting content in places where people are looking. Share your content, your ideas, and yourself with your audience. Share to places where your audience is looking so they can find you.

Finding a way to create content that goes viral and reaches a lot of people can also help with discoverability. If you are creating something that you are sharing, find a way to hook people's attention. Study the media channels. Study other creative content that gets attention. Learn what makes people want to talk about it, and share your ideas with others.

This isn't going to happen when you just introduce yourself to people. Introducing yourself is a good way to get to know someone in real life, but it's not a good way to go viral. Virality is usually connected to some creative idea, some message that touches a nerve or an emotion that people want to share.

Many types of content have the potential to go viral. There are plenty of content formats where you can share your ideas and your messages in a way that has the potential to deliver value to a large audience. Most of it relies on your ability to be creative and tap into the popular themes that are trending on social media. Easier said than done, but virality is a contributing factor to discoverability.

Expand Your Distribution

Distribution is a factor in visibility in that it can expand or limit your capacity to be seen. You must be present in as many places as possible to increase your visibility. If you are only meeting people in person or in one city, then you are limited to those boundaries of your distribution.

If your content only lives on your website or on just one social media channel, like Instagram, then you're missing the opportunity of reaching anyone who uses other channels. The opportunity to be seen is the critical factor.

A lot of people say to focus on one channel first, and not to put yourself everywhere, but that's not a marketing recommendation. It assumes limited experience, limited resources, and limited time and money. It's true that if you have limited resources, you must focus your energy. If you don't have the time or the capability to create good work at a high pace across multiple channels, you need to focus on one.

If you have the time and capability, multiple channels provide a better opportunity to create visibility for your personal brand. The question isn't, *should you do it?* The question is, *when and how do you do it?*

When thinking about distribution, consider the longevity of what you are creating. Some content delivers one-time attention and others deliver recurring attention. One-time attention is what most people create on social media. They create one post, it's potentially seen over the course of a day, then it disappears into the feed. It isn't shown to anyone again. That's how most social media channels are built—to show your thing to a certain amount of people one time and then not again, unless it goes viral.

There are other media channels that are built to create recurring attention. Websites, blogs, YouTube channels, and podcasts are built in a way that categorizes and archives your content. On these media channels, if someone finds you or is searching for a particular topic that you create content about, it won't only send them the newest thing you created but anything you created that is relevant to the thing they're searching for.

The effort you put into creating something that goes into a media channel that emphasizes recurring attention is an opportunity. That's not to say that recurring attention is better than one-time attention. It's just a stronger return on effort. Typically, you need both.

You need one-time attention to continue to give you the opportunity to go viral and be seen by larger audiences. If you reach more people with those one-time attention channels, the goal is to bring them in and convert them into subscribers on channels that you own. Lead them to your other content channels that deliver more recurring attention.

Based on the amount of effort and time you have in each day, developing your process for distribution is the secret to being able to deliver consistently, show up, and be visible more often over time. As you do it more and more often, it starts to add up, and your visibility starts to increase. The opportunity to be seen starts to increase.

Standing out starts with reach, is informed by your discoverability, and is expanded by the opportunity to distribute yourself to as many places as possible.

End of Chapter Questions

Get your worksheet for this chapter at BrandonBirkmeyer.com/FCL.

- Reflect on your current methods of reaching your audience, whether in person or virtually. How can you broaden your reach to connect with more people effectively?

- Consider attending events or conferences where your target audience is likely present. How can you maximize your in-person reach in these settings?

- Are there opportunities to create more content and reach a wider audience through platforms like blogs, YouTube, podcasts, or social media?

- How can you ensure that your content is easily findable by your target audience?

- Are there additional platforms or channels where you could share your content to expand your visibility?

- Where do you want to establish your presence first, and how will you build upon those initial efforts?

Chapter Twenty

LAW #4 Stand Out at the Right Times

O ther than reach, there are two factors that are worth considering when growing the visibility of your personal brand.

Those two factors are:

- frequency – Did someone see your message enough times?

- recency – Did someone see your message at the right time?

Even though your visibility is the number one factor that contributes to you standing out, frequency and recency, are the other variables that can affect your success.

Frequency

Frequency is how often a particular person or audience has the opportunity to see your product. For personal branding, I think of this in terms of the opportunity to see your message, your platform, and you. Every chance you can meet or engage with someone, or you have your ideas and content engage with them, counts toward their overall experience of you as a personal brand.

When thinking about building an audience and standing out in your category, take into consideration how many times you'll have a chance to interact over a long period of time. Think about the person that you're meeting and where you will have an opportunity to engage with them again.

That might mean that you will see them again, in person, at a future event or meeting. Or it might mean that they will encounter you through your website, social media channels, blog posts, emails, or through word-of-mouth. **Every touch point throughout their day is an opportunity for them to interact with you.**

When marketers think about this, they call it the "day in the life" journey of a customer. For every person you meet, think about where they might have the opportunity to interact with you.

- If they're driving to work, they can listen to your podcast.

- If they are at the supermarket and they're scrolling on their phone while they're in line, they can run across the social posts that you've created.

- If they are networking on LinkedIn, they can find an article you wrote, or they might see that you've tagged them in a post.

- When they're checking their emails at night, you are in their inbox.

- When they go to a networking event, they might see you there on stage.

- When talking to a friend, maybe your name will come up in the conversation.

All of these are opportunities for you to be seen again and again by your ideal audience.

The more times that you can engage with someone, the more you have the opportunity for them to choose you. You want to be considered for the opportunity to work together, for a partnership or speaking engagement, or when they are buying a product. There are lots of ways to be chosen, but it starts with being considered. That's the power of frequency.

I think about this a lot in my own business. If I have a guest on my show, not only do I think about their appearance on my show, but I think about the people they could refer me to so they can also be on my show. I think about who they might mention me to as a potential speaker for a guest appearance on a podcast or as a potential client for some work that I'm doing.

Every interaction is an opportunity for someone to experience you. Every interaction helps them to better know you, like you, and trust you. The thing about frequency is that, in a way, it is the opposite of reach. Reach is broad, but frequency is all about focus.

Using the same example from the discussion about reach, let's look at frequency. You have ten people, and you can either meet one person ten times or meet ten people one time. The more effective choice is going to be meeting all ten people one time (focusing on reach, not frequency).

However, the reality is that after you meet those ten people, you might have opportunities to meet them again. And that's the tactic that I see a lot of people skip. Frequency builds over time. You're not trying to race to get in front of the same person a hundred times in one week. **You're trying to build a relationship with them over the long term, and you don't always get to determine what that timeframe looks like.**

Try your best to create more opportunities to meet people a second time and beyond. The opportunity is to create paths for them to choose how frequently they connect with you and see your content.

For example, if you meet someone in person, you can try to connect with them on LinkedIn, and then they may see your posts on LinkedIn more often. In that post, you can mention your email newsletter. They have the choice to subscribe to this email list. In those emails, they see your messages even more often. They are choosing their level of interaction, but you must give them the opportunity to see that.

For others, they may see you once, and then they may not see any of your content until you personally follow up in three weeks or six months, or whatever the timeframe may be.

You must be very deliberate about your frequency in every relationship, and that's on you to determine what relationships deserve what type of frequency. Someone you just met might need more or less frequency at first than someone who has been following you and is now subscribed to your content.

> You can design each of these steps, but be sure to think about the different starting points of your relationships. Someone sees you speak, sees your content online, subscribes to your email list, or hears you in an interview—each of these interactions or starting points should be designed, step-by-step, in terms of the amount of frequency or engagement after that initial contact.

There are triggers along the way that you can set up to determine when to increase or decrease your frequency of contact. Frequency is in your control.

You must decide where to spend your time. Your energy is limited for the things that aren't automated. If you're going to events, choose the right events, and go to as many of them as possible. Don't just choose events to fill your calendar, especially if you don't know who's attending. The power of frequency is in focusing only on the people that are a potential yes for your personal brand and for your business.

Recency

Recency is the opportunity to be seen right before a potential decision, interaction, or engagement. **Recency means being closest to the point of decision-making.**

For example, if you are trying to sell a lot of cars and you know that on a holiday weekend a lot of people go to see cars because they have an extra day off, then you're going to leverage recency.

You're going to run more ads on the Thursday, Friday, and Saturday that lead up to that holiday weekend; more so than seven, eight, or nine days away. The heaviest promotion is going to be right before the holiday weekend. This is true for everything.

They say that when you're throwing an event, even if you announce the event six months out and you have special sales, the majority of the tickets are going to be sold within the last week or two. That's recency coming into play.

It's not just people procrastinating and their inability to decide. A lot of the time, people are thinking about something the most right before they are ready to decide. Your question then becomes, when are you most top of mind for the people you want to be in front of? When is their point of decision, and how can you be in front of them right when that happens?

That may not be the easiest thing to figure out, especially for a personal brand. **To leverage recency, most people figure out some type of schedule.** Look at all three hundred and sixty-five days of the year. You may notice some patterns in your year. There are times when you tend to sell more packages or when people are getting together more often. Those are the times you leverage recency in your promotions and interactions.

For example, a lot of new business planning and initiatives are created in the beginning of the year. So, a lot of goal-setting plans start to happen in December. If you are someone who caters to that, you might offer your goal-setting program in December because you know companies are starting to build their plans out in January.

Or, for gym memberships, they know that people make New Year's resolutions on January 1st. The gyms run ads right before and after that date to take advantage of new gym sign-ups from people who make a resolution to go to the gym at the beginning of the year.

You get to pick and choose when to share your message. When I was in corporate, I would often seek out meetings and lunches with my bosses when it got closer to the timing of my performance review. These were great chances to talk about big projects from the year and big wins.

Now that I work for myself, I still share my wins, but now I share them across social media. It reminds people what I do and how I help. These reminders are critical because most people aren't thinking about you. They are thinking about themselves and it's up to you to remind them of your value.

Figure out what recency looks like for you. List out your holidays. List your own seasonality as well in terms of when you have time to do your work. Write down your key offer windows, and lean into putting more effort around getting your message out about your personal brand at those times.

End of Chapter Questions

Get your worksheet for this chapter at BrandonBirkmeyer.com/FCL.

- How can you adjust your frequency of interaction to create more opportunities for engagement with your audience?

- What steps can you take to design interaction paths that encourage repeated engagement and interaction with your personal brand?

- How can you leverage recency to ensure that your message is seen at the right time, especially during key decision points for your audience?

- What strategies can you implement to ensure that your messages are relevant and compelling, maximizing their impact during key decision moments?

- What steps will you take to enhance your visibility and stand out at the right times?

Chapter Twenty-One

The Confidence Crisis

You could have all the marketing knowledge in the world, but if you don't have the confidence to act, then nothing will happen. Your personal brand is reliant on your energy and your actions.

So, why is it so hard to be confident and take action? Generally, if this was a business or a product, the only thing stopping someone from pressing go on their marketing would be the person who holds the purse strings.

But when it's your personal brand, you are in charge. When it's you standing out as the center of attention, the only thing stopping you is you. The only reason you will stop yourself is a lack of confidence. Confidence is your own security in what you want to offer and tell people about your personal brand. Unfortunately, your reputation is out there, no matter what you do. The question is, do you want to handle your reputation with intention?

Personal branding without intention is just reputation. It's when you add this intention, and you take action, that it starts to become a personal brand. To do that, you must have confidence.

Anyone can create enough confidence to act on their personal brand by following three simple steps.

Number one, know yourself.

Number two, like yourself.

Number three, trust yourself.

Know Yourself

When it comes to personal branding, the fastest way to gain clarity is to ask yourself these four questions:

- What do you want?

- Who are you?

- Where have you been?

- What are you excited about?

The more questions you can ask yourself, the more you will understand the things that are important to you on this personal branding journey, and the better you're going to be at acting and moving forward.

You can't invent your personal brand out of thin air. Your personal brand has been developing all along. It's based on what is truly, authentically, organically you. So, what makes you different?

You probably have more than one thing. Keep track and make a list of your skills. Write down the things that you do well.

All the different facets of your character are potential powers that you can leverage in your personal brand.

Which one you lean into is up to you. But ask yourself the question, what is my superpower? Superpowers can be developed, they can be applied, and you can stop and start them.

After you've started to make a list, pick one or two to lean into as the superpowers you want to be known for. Just pick one word and focus on that as your goal for personal development and growth.

Like Yourself

It's hard to have confidence if you don't like yourself. I know it's a funny thing to say because most of us generally like ourselves. But do you like yourself enough to want to tell other people about you?

You may be shy or polite or humble, and that's great, but managing a personal brand requires you to step out of your comfort zone. **To grow your opportunities, you must find ways to share your brilliance with others.** You can do it in a humble way, but it starts with you being happy about and proud of the things that you've done.

This tends to falter when you start to share things that you are not confident or excited about or that you don't feel like you can take credit for. So, don't share those things. Find things that feel authentic to you.

If you don't have ideas that come from past experience, start by sharing your opinions. You have experiences, history, and ideas that have accumulated over the years of your life. If you're not comfortable sharing those experiences or teaching others, then start with simple expressions of your own opinions and thoughts about things happening around you.

The more you can express your own opinions and thoughts, the more you'll have confidence, and the more you'll like the things you're saying and putting out there.

You're only going to share your ideas if you are excited about them. You might have to express some ideas privately, write them down, journal them, and then only share the ones you're most excited about sharing. Not everything, just those.

If you can find a way to consistently find things to share that you like, that are your ideas, then you will find yourself moving toward more confidence in your personal brand.

Trust Yourself

Trust is a tricky, tricky topic. I've found that when I am most trusting in myself, it's with something that I've accomplished in the past on a consistent basis. It's the things that I'm most comfortable with that I have the most trust in. However, as you are pursuing growth, changing, adapting, and moving toward your future, you will encounter new and uncomfortable things.

So, how do you trust yourself to do things that you've never done before?

You can start by building trust with small accomplishments. Set small, short-term goals that are realistic and achievable. As you commit to those goals and accomplish them, you start to build trust in yourself.

Create a pattern of success. You are establishing a pattern in your mind and showing yourself that you follow through and finish the things that you start.

These patterns can be small things. For example, if you say you're going to make your bed every morning, when you follow through on that, you are proving the worthiness of your own trust. At the end of keeping a promise to yourself for thirty days, you will trust yourself more. However, if you are the type of person who skips some days after you've made that promise, then you will lose trust in yourself. You will say, "Yeah, I can make promises, but I don't always follow through on them."

Building a history that you can trust for any action or behavior is critical in building confidence. Start with actions that matter most to you, and divide them up into very small things. Then make small promises to yourself to act. Give yourself small windows of time to accomplish that action so you can see what that commitment does for you.

As you find and create more wins along the way, celebrate them. Keep track of them. Keep a running history of your wins so that when you look back over time you have proof that you're the type of person that can trust yourself. Also, it feels good to know that there are some wins under your belt because, oftentimes, all we end up seeing are the losses or the failures or the stumbles.

Create a list, review it, and over time, ask yourself what you are proud of that you've accomplished. It's easier to track as you go. Start today. Make a list of commitments and wins along the way. Each week, you can write down what you are proud of from the past week. Find things that you said you would do, and highlight the ones that you accomplish.

Take pride in and celebrate that work and tenacity. And by the end of the year, you'll have fifty-two different items to celebrate that are proof of your performance. Now you have something that is a tool to help you trust yourself and build confidence.

End of Chapter Questions

Get your worksheet for this chapter at BrandonBirkmeyer.com/FCL.

- Where can you increase your presence and engagement in your life? Identify specific situations where you can show up more and participate actively.

- When can you take more initiative and raise your hand? Reflect on situations where you tend to be passive. Identify opportunities to step up, contribute ideas, and drive conversations forward.

- How can you demonstrate leadership in your life? Explore ways in which you can take on leadership roles, whether formally or informally. Consider how you can set a vision, make decisions, and foster collaboration.

- How can you enhance your knowledge and proficiency in your organization's tools and systems? Consider ways to improve your understanding of the tools and systems used within your organization.

Chapter Twenty-Two

Stepping Up and Standing Out

T here are three questions you can ask yourself that will help you to create your plan for taking action and becoming more front and center in your life:

Where can you be more present?

The goal is to move from absent to present. Where in your life can you show up more often? Whether it's in meetings, in day-to-day life, in conversations, in client opportunities, or in extracurricular opportunities, where can you be more present? That means showing up in more places, and while you're there, being more engaged in the conversation.

When can you raise your hand?

This is where we move from passive to active. Look for places to raise your hand, and be the first person to contribute to a conversation. Find ways to participate more actively, drive the conversation with your ideas, and practice leadership—engaging clients and your peers. Step out of your routine, and start to build a plan for taking more initiative and being more front and center in your life.

How can you lead?

How do you go from follower to leader? How can you lead a follower? A leader finds a way to set the vision and mission for the group, to take charge, to make decisions, to create unity and collaboration amongst the team, and to drive the plan forward. So, where can you raise your hand; then, how can you lead?

Leadership can take many forms. Leadership can be in a meeting or on a project, but it can also be in your daily life. Where can you lead in terms of ideas, in terms of relationships, and in terms of activity and participation? Where can you take a leadership role?

Come up with new ideas that you can present to your organization. Be a leader in terms of training and bringing others along on their journey.

Answer the question for yourself. *How can you be more front and center? How can you lead?*

Ready to get started? Take our personal branding quiz/scorecard. Go to BrandonBirkmeyer.com/FCL.

CONCLUSION

A nytime I get stuck, it's usually because I'm thinking instead of acting. If you are feeling stuck, it's time to shake things up and try something new. You may fail, but even failure adds clarity.

You don't have to have it all figured out in the beginning. In fact, you won't have any of it figured out. You just need to know the direction in which you are heading and where to start. You must have the courage to start and keep starting every day.

I built this book as a roadmap, but the map does not have a final destination because there isn't one. **Your personal brand will always be a work in progress.** And as you step into the role of leadership, you will find new challenges and new journeys.

Leadership is also not a destination. Your leadership journey will change as you change. Your growth as a person contributes to your growth as a leader. My intention is to give you the motivation to push yourself to grow.

It's easy to get comfortable, which is why the first steps in this roadmap involve finding ways to get out of your comfort zone—breaking free from your routines and habits. This book is a wake-up call, reminding you to pay attention to the journey you are on.

I hope you wake up every day and remind yourself to be front and center in your actions. Seek out opportunities to step up with courage and enthusiasm so that you are an engaged participant and leader in your life. Become highly aware of the right times and places to share your message and get the visibility and recognition you deserve.

If you get lost or aren't sure what's next on your path, take a look at this roadmap and think about the three actions you can take on your journey: creating content, building community, and making an impact.

These actions will always provide a path forward. There will always be new ideas to share that help establish your authority. There will always be people to meet and relationships to nurture that build your influence. And there will always be new problems to solve and new ways to be of service that create value.

Your front and center journey has already started. It starts every time you get curious and wonder. Your curiosity is the compass that guides you on this path. The journey must matter to you for it to be a path worth walking. If you are curious about it, it's because it matters to you, whether you know it or not. Listen to that curiosity, and follow where it leads you.

ABOUT THE AUTHOR

BRANDON BIRKMEYER is a former Coca-Cola and Apple media director with over twenty years of experience in marketing at the Big Five advertising agencies in New York City and Los Angeles advising top FORTUNE 100 companies on brand strategy. Brandon also produces and hosts a top-five branding podcast and YouTube channel called *Brands On Brands*.

In 2024, Brandon wrote *Front & Center Leadership* to help corporate employees, creators, and entrepreneurs stop getting overlooked and start using their personal brand to stand out in their lives and businesses. Brandon is now a sought-after consultant, coach, author, speaker, and facilitator and he has a BBA from Loyola Marymount University in California.

Brandon moved from Los Angeles, California to Raleigh, North Carolina in 2021 to pursue his dream of being a cool suburban dad to his two kids and trophy husband to his wife, Jema. It's still a work in progress.

For more information go to BrandonBirkmeyer.com.

www.ingramcontent.com/pod-product-compliance
Lightning Source LLC
Chambersburg PA
CBHW020236130626
46549CB00005B/1920